D0705745

Proof of the Apostolic Preaching

Irenaeus

Copyright © 2015 Beloved Publishing

All rights reserved. No part of this book may be reproduced, scanned, or distributed in any printed or electronic form without permission.

Printed in the United States of America

ISBN:1631741144

1. Knowing, my beloved Marcianus, your desire to walk in godliness, which alone leads man to life eternal, I rejoice with you and make my prayer that you may preserve your faith entire and so be pleasing to God who made you. Would that it were possible for us to be always together, to help each other and to lighten the labour of our earthly life by continual discourse together on the things that profit.[1] But, since at this present time we are parted from one another in the body, yet according to our power we will not fail to speak with you a little by writing, and to show forth in brief the preaching of the truth for the confirmation of your faith.[2] We send you as it were a manual of essentials,[3] that by little you may attain to much, learning in short space all the members of the body of the truth, and receiving in brief the |70 demonstration of the things of God. So shall it be fruitful to your own salvation, and you shall put to shame all who inculcate falsehood, and bring with all confidence our sound and pure teaching to everyone who desires to understand it. For one is the way leading upwards for all who see, lightened with heavenly light: but many and dark and contrary are the ways of them that see not. This way leads to the kingdom of heaven, uniting man to God: but those ways bring down to death, separating man from God. Wherefore it is needful for you and for all who care for their own salvation to make your course unswerving, firm and sure by means of faith, that you falter not, nor be retarded and detained in material desires, nor turn aside and wander from the right.

2. Now, since man is a living being compounded of soul and flesh, he must needs exist by both of these: and, whereas from both of them offences come, purity of the flesh is the restraining abstinence from all shameful things and all unrighteous deeds, and purity of the soul is the keeping faith towards God entire, neither adding thereto nor diminishing therefrom. For godliness is obscured and dulled by the soiling and the staining of the flesh, and is broken and polluted and no more entire, if falsehood enter into the soul: but it will keep itself in its. beauty and its measure, when truth is constant in the soul[4] and purity in the flesh. For what |71 profit is it to know the truth in words, and to pollute the flesh and perform the works of evil? Or what profit can purity of the flesh bring, if truth be not in the soul?

For these rejoice with one another, and are united and allied to bring man face to face with God. Wherefore the Holy Spirit says by David: *Blessed is the man who hath not walked in the counsel of the ungodly:*[8] that is, the counsel of the nations which know not God: for those are ungodly who worship not the God that truly is. And therefore the Word says to Moses: *I am He that is:*[5][9] but they that worship not the God that is, these are the ungodly. *And hath not stood in the way of sinners:* but sinners are those who have the knowledge of God and keep not His commandments; that is, disdainful scorners. *And hath not sat in the seat of the pestilential:*[6] now the pestilential are those who by wicked and perverse doctrines corrupt not themselves only, but others also. For the seat is a symbol of teaching. Such then are all heretics: they sit in the seats of the pestilential, and those are corrupted who receive the venom of their doctrine.

3. Now, that we may not suffer ought of this kind, we must needs hold the rule of the faith without deviation,[7] and do the commandments of God, believing in God and fearing Him as Lord and loving Him as Father. Now this doing is produced |72 by faith: for Isaiah says: *If ye believe not, neither shall ye understand.*[10] And faith is produced by the truth; for faith rests on things that truly are. For in things that are, as they are, we believe; and believing in things that are, as they ever are, we keep firm our confidence in them. Since then faith is the perpetuation of our salvation, we must needs bestow much pains on the maintenance thereof, in order that we may have a true comprehension of the things that are. Now faith occasions this for us; even as the Elders, the disciples of the Apostles, have handed down to us. First of all it bids us bear in mind that we have received baptism for the remission of sins, in the name of God the Father, and in the name of Jesus Christ, the Son of God, who was incarnate and died and rose again, and in the Holy Spirit of God. And that this baptism is the seal of eternal life, and is the new birth unto God, that we should no longer be the sons of mortal men, but of the eternal and perpetual God; and that what is everlasting and continuing is made God;[11] and is over all things that are made, and all things are put under Him; |73 and all the things that are put under Him are made His own; for God is not ruler and Lord over the things of another,

but over His own;[12] and all things are God's; and therefore God is Almighty, and all things are of God.

4. For it is necessary that things that are made should have the beginning of their making from some great cause; and the beginning of all things is God. For He Himself was not made by any, and by Him all things were made. And therefore it is right first of all to believe that there is One God, the Father, who made and fashioned all things, and made what was not that it should be, and who, containing all things, alone is uncontained.[13] Now among all things is this world of ours, and in the world is man: so then this world also was formed by God.

5. Thus then there is shown forth [14] One God, the Father, not made, invisible, creator of all things; above whom there is no other God, and after whom there is no other God.[15] And, since God is rational, | 74 therefore by (the) Word He created the things that were made;[16] and God is Spirit, and by (the) Spirit He adorned all things: as also the prophet says: *By the word of the Lord were the heavens established, and by his spirit all their power.*[17] Since then the Word establishes, that is to say, gives body [18] and grants the reality of being, and the Spirit gives order and form to the diversity of the powers; rightly and fittingly is the Word called the Son, and the Spirit the Wisdom of God. Well also does Paul His apostle say: *One God, the Father, who is over all and through all and in us all.*[19] For *over all* is the Father; and *through all* is the Son, for through Him all things were made by the Father; and *in us all* is the Spirit, who cries *Abba Father,*[20] and fashions man into the likeness of God.[4] Now the Spirit shows forth the Word, and therefore the prophets announced the Son of God; and the Word utters the Spirit, and therefore is Himself the announcer of the prophets, and leads and draws man to the Father.

6. This then is the order of the rule of our faith, and the foundation of the building, and the |75 stability of our conversation: God, the Father, not made, not material, invisible; one God, the creator of all things: this is the first point[21] of our faith. The second point is: The Word of God, Son of God, Christ Jesus our Lord, who was manifested to the prophets according to the form of their

prophesying and according to the method of the dispensation of the Father:[22] through whom all things were made; who also at the end of the times, to complete and gather up[23] all things, was made man among men, visible and tangible,[24] in order to abolish death and show forth life and produce a community of union between God and man. And the third point is: The Holy Spirit, through whom the prophets prophesied, and the fathers learned the things of God, and the righteous were led forth into the way of righteousness; and who in the end of the times was poured out in a new way upon mankind in all the earth, renewing man unto God.

7. And for this reason the baptism of our |76 regeneration proceeds through these three points: God the Father bestowing on us regeneration through His Son by the Holy Spirit. For as many as carry (in them) the Spirit of God are led to the Word, that is to the Son; and the Son brings them to the Father; and the Father causes them to possess incorruption. Without the Spirit it is not possible to behold the Word of God, nor without the Son can any draw near to the Father: for the knowledge of the Father is the Son, and the knowledge of the Son of God is through the Holy Spirit; and, according to the good pleasure of the Father, the Son ministers and dispenses the Spirit to whomsoever the Father wills and as He wills.

8. And by the Spirit the Father is called Most High and Almighty and Lord of hosts; that we may learn concerning God that He it is who is creator of heaven and earth and all the world, and maker of angels and men, and Lord of all, through whom all things exist and by whom all things are sustained; merciful, compassionate and very tender, good, just, the God of all, both of Jews and of Gentiles, and of them that believe. To them that believe He is as Father, for in the end of the times He opened up the covenant of adoption; |77 but to the Jews as Lord and Lawgiver, for in the intermediate times, when man forgat God and departed and revolted from Him, He brought them into subjection by the Law, that they might learn that they had for Lord the maker and creator, who also gives the breath of life, and whom we ought to worship day and night: and to the Gentiles as maker and creator and almighty: and to all alike sustainer and nourisher and king and judge; for none shall escape and be delivered

from His judgment, neither Jew nor Gentile, nor believer that has sinned, nor angel: but they who now reject His goodness shall know His power in judgment, according to that which the blessed apostle says: *Not knowing that the goodness of God leadeth thee to repentance; but according to thy hardness and impenitent heart thou treasurest up for thyself wrath in the day of wrath and of the revelation of the righteous judgment of God, who shall render to every man according to his works.*[25] This is He who is called in the Law the God of Abraham and the God of Isaac and the God of Jacob, the God of the living; although the sublimity and greatness of this God is unspeakable.

9. Now this world is encompassed by seven heavens,[26] in which dwell powers and angels and |78 archangels, doing service to God, the Almighty and Maker of all things: not as though He was in need, but that they may not be idle and unprofitable and ineffectual.[27] Wherefore also the Spirit of God is manifold in (His) indwelling,[28] and in seven forms of service [29] is He reckoned by the prophet Isaiah, as resting on the Son of God, that is the Word, in His coming as man. *The Spirit of God,* he says, *shall rest upon him, the Spirit of wisdom and of understanding, the Spirit of counsel and of might, (the Spirit of knowledge) and of godliness; the Spirit of the fear of God shall fill him.*[30] Now the heaven which is first from above,[31] and encompasses the rest, is (that of) wisdom; and the |79 second from it, of understanding; and the third, of counsel; and the fourth, reckoned from above, (is that) of might; and the fifth, of knowledge; and the sixth, of godliness; and the seventh, this firmament of ours, is full of the fear of that Spirit which gives light to the heavens. For, as the pattern (of this), Moses received the seven-branched candlestick, that shined continually in the holy place; for as a pattern of the heavens he received this service, according to that which the Word spake unto him: *Thou shalt make (it) according to all the pattern of the things which thou hast seen in the mount.*[32]

10. Now this God is glorified by His Word who is His Son continually,[33] and by the Holy Spirit who is the Wisdom of the Father of all: and the power(s) of these, (namely) of the Word and Wisdom, which are called Cherubim and Seraphim,[34] with unceasing voices glorify God; and |80 every created thing that is in the heavens

offers glory to God the Father of all.[35] He by His Word has created the whole world, and in the world are the angels; and to all the world He has given laws wherein each several thing should abide, and according to that which is determined by God should not pass their bounds, each fulfilling his appointed task.

11. But man He formed with His own hands,[36] taking from the earth that which was purest and finest, and mingling in measure His own power with the earth. For He traced His own form on the formation, [37] that that which should 'be seen should be of divine form: for (as) the image of God was man formed and set on the earth. And that he might become living, He breathed on his face the breath of life; that both for the breath and for the formation man should be like unto God. Moreover he was free and self-controlled, being made by God for this end, that he might rule all those things that were upon the earth. And this great created world, prepared by God before the formation of man, was given to man as his place, containing all things within itself.[38] And there were in this place also with (their) tasks the | 81 servants of that God who formed all things; and the steward, who was set over all his fellow-servants received this place. Now the servants were angels, and the steward was the archangel.[39]

12. Now, having made man lord of the earth and all things in it, He secretly appointed him lord also of those who were servants in it. They however were in their perfection; but the lord, that is, man, was (but) small; for he was a child; and it was necessary that he should grow, and so come to (his) perfection. And, that he might have his nourishment and growth with festive and dainty meats, He prepared him a place better than this world,[40] excelling in air, beauty, light, food, plants, |82 fruit, water, and all other necessaries of life: and its name is Paradise. And so fair and good was this Paradise, that the Word of God continually resorted thither, and walked and talked with the man, figuring beforehand the things that should be in the future, (namely) that He should dwell with him and talk with him, and should be with men, teaching them righteousness. But man was a child, not yet having his understanding perfected; wherefore also he was easily led astray by the deceiver.

13. And, whilst man dwelt in Paradise, God brought before him all living things and commanded him to give names to them all; *and whatsoever Adam called a living soul, that was its name.*[41] And He determined also to make a helper for the man: for thus God said, *It is not good for the man to be alone: let us make for him a helper meet for him.*[42] For among all the other living things there was not found a helper equal and comparable and like to Adam. But God Himself *cast a trance upon Adam and made him sleep;*[43] and, that work might be accomplished from work, since there was no sleep in Paradise, this was brought upon Adam by the will of God; and God *took one of Adam's ribs and filled up the flesh in its place, and the rib which He took He builded into a woman;* [44] *and so He brought her to Adam;* and he seeing (her) said: *This is now bone of my bone, flesh of my flesh: she shall be called woman, because she was taken from her husband.* |83

14. And Adam and Eve----for that is the name of the woman----*were naked, and were not ashamed;*[45] for there was in them an innocent and childlike mind, and it was not possible for them to conceive and understand anything of that which by wickedness through lusts and shameful desires is born in the soul. For they were at that time entire, preserving their own nature; since they had the breath of life which was breathed on their creation: and, while this breath remains in its place and power, it has no comprehension and understanding of things that are base. And therefore they were not ashamed, kissing and embracing each other in purity after the manner of children.

15. But, lest man should conceive thoughts too high, and be exalted and uplifted, as though he had no lord, because of the authority and freedom granted to him, and so should transgress against his maker God, overpassing his measure, and entertain selfish imaginings of pride in opposition to God; a law was given to him by God, in order that he might perceive that he had as lord the Lord of all. And He set him certain limitations, so that, if he should keep the commandment of God, he should ever remain such as he was, that is to say, immortal; but, if he should not keep it, he should become mortal and be dissolved to earth from whence his formation had been taken. Now the commandment was this: *Of every tree that is in the Paradise thou shalt freely eat; but of that tree alone from which is the knowledge of*

good |84 and evil, of it thou shalt not eat; for in the day thou eatest, thou shalt surely die.[46]

16. This commandment the man kept not, but was disobedient to God, being led astray by the angel who, for the great gifts of God which He had given to man, was envious and jealous of him,[47] and both brought himself to nought and made man sinful, persuading him to disobey the commandment of God. So the angel, becoming by his falsehood the author and originator of sin, himself was struck down, having offended against God, and man he caused to be cast out from Paradise. And, because through the guidance of his disposition he apostatized and departed from God, he was called Satan, according to the Hebrew word; that is, Apostate: [48] but he is also called Slanderer. Now God cursed the serpent which carried and conveyed the Slanderer; and this malediction came on the beast himself and on the angel hidden and concealed in him, even on Satan; and man He put away from His presence, removing him and making him to dwell on the way to Paradise [49] at that time; because Paradise receiveth not the sinful.

17. And when they were put out of Paradise, Adam and his wife Eve fell into many troubles of anxious grief, going about with sorrow and toil |85 and lamentation in this world. For under the beams of this sun man tilled the earth, and it put forth thorns and thistles, the punishment of sin. Then was fulfilled that which was written: *Adam knew his wife, and she conceived and bare Cain;*[50] and after him *she bare Abel,* Now the apostate angel, who led man into disobedience and made him sinful and caused his expulsion from Paradise, not content with the first evil, wrought a second on the brothers; for filling Cain with his spirit he made him a fratricide. And so Abel died, slain by his brother; signifying thenceforth that certain should be persecuted and oppressed and slain, the unrighteous slaying and persecuting the righteous. And upon this God was angered yet more, and cursed Cain; and it came to pass that everyone of that race in successive generations was made like to the begetter. And God *raised up* another son to Adam, *instead of Abel* who was slain.[51]

18. And for a very long while wickedness extended and spread, and reached and laid hold upon the whole race of mankind, until a very small seed of righteousness remained among them: and illicit unions took place upon the earth, since angels were united with the daughters of the race of mankind; and they bore to them sons who for their exceeding greatness were called giants. And the angels brought as presents to their wives teachings of wickedness,[52] in that they brought |86 them the virtues of roots and herbs, dyeing in colours and cosmetics, the discovery of rare substances, love-potions, aversions, amours, concupiscence, constraints of love, spells of bewitchment, and all sorcery and idolatry hateful to God; by the entry of which things into the world evil extended and spread, while righteousness was diminished and enfeebled.

19. Until judgment came upon the world from God by means of a flood, in the tenth generation from the first-formed (man); Noah alone being found righteous. And he for his righteousness was himself delivered, and his wife and his three sons, and the three wives of his sons, being shut up in the ark. And when destruction came upon all, both man and also animals, that were upon the earth, that which was preserved in the ark escaped. Now the three sons of Noah were Shem, Ham and Japheth, from whom again the race was multiplied: for these were the beginning of mankind after the flood.

20. Now of these one fell under a curse, and the two (others) inherited a blessing by reason of their works. For the younger of them,[53] who was called Ham, having mocked his father, and having been |87 condemned of the sin of impiety because of his outrage and unrighteousness against his father, received a curse; and all the posterity that came of him he involved in the curse; whence it came about that his whole race after him were accursed, and in sins they increased and multiplied. But Shem and Japheth, his brothers, because of their piety towards their father obtained a blessing. Now the curse of Ham, wherewith his father Noah cursed him, is this: *Cursed be Ham the child;* [54] *a servant shall he be unto his brethren.*[55] This having come upon his race, he begat many descendants upon the earth, (even) for fourteen generations, growing up in a wild condition; and then his race was cut off by God, being delivered up

to judgment. For the Canaanites and Hittites and Peresites and Hivites and Amorites and Jebusites and Gergasites and Sodomites, the Arabians also and the dwellers in Phoenicia, all the Egyptians and the Libyans,[56] are of the posterity of Ham, who have fallen under the curse; for the curse is of long duration over the ungodly.

21. And even as the curse passed on, so also the blessing passed on to the race of him who was |88 blessed, to each in his own order. For first of them was Shem blessed in these words: *Blessed be the Lord, the God of Shem; and Ham* [57] *shall be his servant.*[58] The power of the blessing lies in this, that the God and Lord of all should be to Shem a peculiar possession of worship. And the blessing extended and reached unto Abraham, who was reckoned as descended in the tenth generation from the race of Shem: and therefore the Father and God of all was pleased to be called the God of Abraham and the God of Isaac and the God of Jacob; because the blessing of Shem reached out and attached itself to Abraham. Now the blessing of Japheth is on this wise: *God shall enlarge unto Japheth, and he shall dwell in the house of Shem, and Ham* [59] *shall be his servant.*[60] That is to say: In the end of the ages he blossomed forth, at the appearing of the Lord, through the calling of the Gentiles, when God enlarged unto them the calling; and *their sound went out into all the earth, and their words to the end of the world.*[61] The enlarging, then, is the calling from among the Gentiles, that is to say, the Church.[62] *And he dwells in the house* |89 *of Shem;* that is, in the inheritance of the fathers, receiving in Christ Jesus the right of the firstborn. So in the rank in which each was blessed, in that same order through his posterity he received the fruit of the blessing.[63]

22. Now after the Flood God made a covenant with all the world, even with every living thing of animals and of men, that He would no more destroy with a flood all that grew upon the earth. And He set them a sign (saying): *When the sky shall be covered with a cloud, the bow shall be seen in the cloud; and I will remember my covenant, and will no more destroy by water every moving thing upon the earth.*[64] And He changed the food of men, giving them leave to eat flesh: for from Adam the first-formed until the Flood men ate only of seeds and the fruit of trees, and to eat flesh was not permitted to them. But since

the three sons of Noah were the beginning of a race of men, God blessed them for multiplication and increase, saying: *Increase and multiply, and replenish the earth and rule it; and the fear and dread of you shall be upon every living thing of animals and upon all the fowls of the air; and they shall be to you for meat, even as the green herb: but the flesh with the blood of life ye shall not eat: for your blood also will I require at the hand of all beasts and at the hand of man. Whoso sheddeth a man's blood, in return for his blood shall it be shed.*[65] For He made man the |90 image of God; and the image of God is the Son, after whose image man was made: and for this cause He appeared in the end of the times that He might show the image (to be) like unto Himself. According to this covenant the race of man multiplied, springing up from the seed of the three. And *upon the earth was one lip,* that is to say one language.[66]

23. And they arose and came from the land of the east; and, as they went through the land, they chanced upon the land of Shinar, which was exceeding broad; where they took in hand to build a tower. They sought means thereby to go up to heaven, and be able to leave their work as a memorial to those men who should come after them. And the building was made with burnt bricks and bitumen: and the boldness of their audacity went forward, as they were all of one mind and consent, and by means of one speech they served the purpose of their desires. But that the work should advance no further, God divided their tongues, that they should no longer be able to understand one another. And so they were scattered and planted out, and took possession of the world, and dwelt in groups and companies each according to his language: whence came the diverse tribes and various languages upon the earth. So then, whereas three races of men took possession of the earth, and one of them was under the curse, and two under the blessing, the blessing first of all came to Shem, whose |91 race dwelt in the east and held the land of the Chaldeans.

24. In process of time, that is to say, in the tenth generation after the Flood, Abraham appeared,[67] seeking for the God who by the blessing of his ancestor was due and proper to him.[68] And when, urged by the eagerness of his spirit, he went all about the world, searching where God is, and failed to find out; God took pity on him who alone was

silently seeking Him; and He appeared unto *Abraham,* making Himself known by the Word, as by a beam of light. For He spake with him from heaven, and said unto him: *Get thee out of thy country, and from thy kindred, and from thy father's house; and come into the land that I will show thee,*[69] and there dwell. And he believed the heavenly voice, being then of ripe age, even seventy [70] years old, and having a wife; and together with her he went forth from Mesopotamia, taking with him Lot, the son of his brother who was dead. And when he came into the land which now is called Judaea, in which at that time dwelt seven tribes descended from Ham, God appeared unto him in a vision and said: *To thee will I give this land, and to thy seed after thee, for an everlasting possession,*[71] and (He said) that his seed should be a stranger in a land not their own, and should be evil-entreated there, being afflicted and |92 in bondage four hundred years; and in the fourth generation should return unto the place that was promised to Abraham; and that God would judge that race which had brought his seed into bondage. And, that Abraham might know as well the multitude as the glory of his seed, God brought him forth abroad by night, and said: *Look upon the heaven, and behold the stars of the heaven, if thou be able to number them: so shall thy seed be.*[72] And when God saw the undoubting and unwavering certainty of his spirit, He bare witness unto him by the Holy Spirit, saying in the Scripture: *And Abraham believed, and it was counted unto him for righteousness.*[73] And he was uncircumcised when this witness was borne; and, that the excellency of his faith should be made known by a sign, He gave him circumcision, *a seal of the righteousness* [74] *of that faith which he had in uncircumcision.*[75] And after this there was born to him a son, Isaac, from Sarah who was barren, according to the promise of God; and him he circumcised, according to that which God had covenanted with him. And of Isaac was Jacob born; and on this wise the original blessing of Shem reached to Abraham, and from Abraham to Isaac, and from Isaac to Jacob, the inheritance of the Spirit being imparted to them: for He was called the God of Abraham and the God of Isaac and the God of Jacob. And Jacob begat twelve sons, from whom the twelve tribes of Israel were named. 25. And when famine had come upon all the |93 earth, it chanced that in Egypt alone there was food; and Jacob with all his seed removed and dwelt in Egypt: and the number of all that migrated was *threescore and fifteen souls:*[76] and in four hundred years, as the oracle had declared beforehand, they became six hundred and sixty thousand. And, because they were grievously afflicted and oppressed through evil bondage, and sighed and groaned unto God, the God of their fathers, Abraham and Isaac and Jacob; He brought them out of Egypt by the hand of Moses and Aaron, smiting the Egyptians with ten plagues, and in the last plague sending a destroying angel and slaying their first-born, both of man and of beast: wherefrom He saved the children of Israel, revealing in a mystery the sufferings of Christ by the sacrifice of a lamb without spot, and giving its blood to be smeared on the houses of the Hebrews as a sure precaution. And the name of this mystery is Passion,[77] the source of deliverance. And dividing the Red Sea, He brought the children of Israel with all security to the wilderness; and as to the pursuing Egyptians, who followed them and entered into the sea, they were all overwhelmed; this judgment of God coming upon those who had iniquitously oppressed the seed of Abraham.

26. And in the wilderness Moses received the Law from God, *the Ten Words on tables of stone, written with the finger of God* [78] (now the finger of |94 God is that which is stretched forth from the Father in the Holy Spirit);[79] and the commandments and ordinances which he delivered to the children of Israel to observe. And the tabernacle of witness he constructed by the command of God, the visible form on earth of those things which are spiritual and invisible in the heavens, and a figure of the form of the Church, and a prophecy of things to come: in which also were the vessels and the altars of sacrifice and the ark in which he placed the tables (of the Law). And he appointed as priests Aaron and his sons, assigning the priesthood to all their tribe: and they were of the seed of Levi. Moreover this whole tribe he summoned by the word of God to accomplish the work of service in the temple of God, and gave them the Levitical law, (to shew) what and what manner of men they ought to be who are continually employed in performing the service of the temple of God.

27. And when they were near to the land, which God had promised to Abraham and his seed, Moses chose a man from every tribe, and

sent them to search out the land and the cities therein and the dwellers in the cities. At that time God revealed to him the Name which alone is able to save them that believe thereon; and Moses changed the name of Oshea the son of Nun, one of them that were sent, and named him Jesus:[80] and so he |95 sent them forth with the power of the Name, believing that he should receive them back safe and sound through the guidance of the Name: which came to pass.[81] Now when they had gone and searched and enquired, they returned bringing with them a bunch of grapes; and some of the twelve who were sent cast the whole multitude into fear and dismay, saying that the cities were exceeding great and walled, and the sons of the giants dwelt therein, so that it was (not) possible for them to take the land. And thereupon it fell out that all the multitude wept, failing to believe that it was God who should grant them power and subjugate all to them. And they spake evil also of the land, as not being good, and as though it were not worth while to undergo the danger for the sake of such a land. But two of the twelve, Jesus the son of Nun, and Caleb the son of Jephunneh, rent their clothes for the evil that was done, and besought the people not to be disheartened nor lose their courage; for God had given all into their hands, and the land was exceeding good. And when they believed not, but the people still continued in the same unbelief, God changed and altered their way, that they should wander desolate and sore smitten in the desert. And according to the days that they were in going and returning who had spied out the land----and these were forty in number----setting a |96 year for a day, He kept them in the wilderness for the space of forty years; and none of those who were fullgrown and had understanding counted He worthy to enter into the land because of their unbelief, save only the two who had testified of the inheritance, Jesus the son of Nun and Caleb the son of Jephunneh, and those who were quite young and knew not the right hand and the left. So all the unbelieving multitude perished and were consumed in the wilderness, receiving one by one the due reward of their want of faith: but the children, growing up in the course of forty years, filled up the number of the dead.

28. When the forty years were fulfilled, the people drew near to the Jordan, and were assembled and arrayed over against Jericho. Here Moses gathered the people together, and summed up all afresh, proclaiming the mighty works of God even unto that day, fashioning and preparing those that had grown up in the wilderness to fear God and keep His commandments, imposing on them as it were a new legislation, adding to that which was made before. And this was called Deuteronomy:[82] and in it were written many prophecies concerning our Lord Jesus Christ and concerning the people, and also concerning the calling of the Gentiles and concerning the kingdom.

29. And, when Moses had finished his course, |97 it was said to him by God: *Get thee up into the mountain, and die*:[83] for thou shalt not bring in my people into the land. So he *died according to the word of the Lord*;[84] and Jesus the son of Nun succeeded him. He divided the Jordan and made the people to pass over into the land; and, when he had overthrown and destroyed the seven races that dwelt therein, he assigned to the people the temporal Jerusalem,[85] wherein David was king, and Solomon his son, who builded the temple to the name of God, according to the likeness of the tabernacle which had been made by Moses after the pattern of the heavenly and spiritual things.

30. Hither were the prophets sent by God through the Holy Spirit; and they instructed the people and turned them to the God of their fathers, the Almighty; and they became heralds of the revelation of our Lord Jesus Christ the Son of God, declaring that from the posterity of David His flesh should blossom forth; that after the flesh He might be the son of David, who was the son of Abraham by a long succession; but according to the spirit Son of God, pre-existing[86] with the Father, begotten before all the creation of the world, and at the end of the times appearing to all the world as man, the Word of God *gathering up* in Himself *all things that are in heaven and that are on earth*.[87]

31. So then He united man with God, and established a community of union [88] between God |98 and man; since we could not in any other way participate in incorruption, save by His coming among us. For so long as incorruption was invisible and unrevealed, it helped us

not at all: therefore it became visible,[89] that in all respects we might participate in the reception of incorruption. And, because in the original formation of Adam all of us were tied and bound up with death through his disobedience, it was right that through the obedience of Him who was made man for us we should be released from death: and because death reigned over the flesh, it was right that through the flesh it should lose its force and let man go free from its oppression. So *the Word was made flesh,*[90] that, through that very flesh which sin had ruled and dominated, it should lose its force and be no longer in us. And therefore our Lord took that same original formation as (His) entry into flesh, so that He might draw near and contend on behalf of the fathers, and conquer by Adam that which by Adam had stricken us down.

32. Whence then is the substance of the first-formed (man)? From the Will and the Wisdom |99 of God, and from the virgin earth.[91] *For God had not sent rain,* the Scripture says, *upon the earth,* before man was made; *and there was no man to till the earth.*[92] From this, then, whilst it was still virgin, God took dust of the earth and formed the man, the beginning of mankind. So then the Lord, summing up afresh this man, took the same dispensation of entry into flesh, being born from the Virgin by the Will and the Wisdom of God; that He also should show forth the likeness of Adam's entry into flesh,[2] and there should be that which was written in the beginning, *man after the image and likeness* of God.[93]

33. And just as through a disobedient virgin man was stricken down and fell into death, so through the Virgin who was obedient to the Word of God man was reanimated and received life.[94] For the Lord came to seek again the sheep that |100 was lost;[95] and man it was that was lost: and for this cause there was not made some other formation, but in that same which had its descent from Adam He preserved the likeness of the (first) formation.[96] For it was necessary that Adam should be summed up in Christ, that mortality might be swallowed up and overwhelmed by immortality; and Eve summed up in Mary, that a virgin should be a virgin's intercessor, and by a virgin's obedience undo and put away the disobedience of a virgin.[97]

34. And the trespass which came by the tree was undone by the tree of obedience, when, hearkening unto God, the Son of man was nailed to the tree; thereby putting away the knowledge of evil and bringing in and establishing the knowledge of good: now evil it is to disobey God, even as hearkening unto God is good. And for this cause the Word spake by Isaiah the prophet, announcing beforehand that which was to come----for therefore are they prophets, because they proclaim what is to come: by him then spake the Word thus: |101 *I refuse not, nor gainsay: I gave my back to scourging, and my cheeks to smiting;*[98] *and my face I turned not away from the shame of spitting.*[99] So then by the obedience wherewith He obeyed *even unto death,*[100] hanging on the tree, He put away the old disobedience which was wrought in the tree. Now seeing that He is the Word of God Almighty, who in unseen wise in our midst is universally extended in all the world, and encompasses its length and breadth and height and depth [101]----for by the Word of God the whole universe is ordered and disposed----in it is crucified the Son of God, inscribed crosswise upon it all:[102] for it is right that He being made visible, should set upon all things visible the sharing of His cross, that He might show His operation on visible things through a visible form. For He it is who illuminates the height, that is the heavens; and encompasses the deep which is beneath the earth; and stretches and spreads out the length from east to west; and steers across the breadth of north and south; |102 summoning all that are scattered in every quarter to the knowledge of the Father.

35. Moreover He fulfilled the promise made to Abraham, which God had promised him, to make his seed as the stars of heaven. For this Christ did, who was born of the Virgin who was of Abraham's seed, and constituted those who have faith in Him *lights in the world,*[1] and by the same faith with Abraham justified the Gentiles. For *Abraham believed God, and it was counted unto him for righteousness.* In like manner we also are justified by faith in God: for *the just shall live by faith.* Now *not by the law is the promise to Abraham, but by faith:* for Abraham was justified by faith: and *for a righteous man the law is not made.* In like manner we also are justified not by the law, but by faith,

which is witnessed to in the law and in the prophets, whom the Word of God presents to us.[103]

36. And He fulfilled the promise to David; for to him God had promised that *of the fruit of his body* He would raise up an eternal King,[104] whose kingdom should have no end. And this King is Christ, the Son of God, who became the Son of man; that is, who became the fruit of that Virgin who had her descent from David. And for this cause |103 the promise was, *Of the fruit of thy body* [105]----that He might declare the peculiar uniqueness of Him, who was the fruit of the virgin body that was of David, (even of Him) who was King over the house of David, (and) of whose kingdom there shall be no end.

37. Thus then He gloriously achieved our redemption, and fulfilled the promise of the fathers, and abolished the old disobedience. The Son of God became Son of David and Son of Abraham; perfecting and summing up this in Himself, that He might make us to possess life. The Word of God was made flesh by the dispensation of the Virgin, to abolish death and make man live. For we were imprisoned by sin, being born in sinfulness and living under death.

38. But God the Father was very merciful: He sent His creative [106] Word, who in coming to deliver us came to the very place and spot in which we had lost life, and brake the bonds of our fetters. And His light appeared and made the darkness of the prison disappear, and hallowed our birth and destroyed death, loosing those same fetters in which we were enchained. And He manifested |104 the resurrection, [107] Himself becoming *the first-begotten of the dead,*[108] and in Himself raising up man that was fallen, lifting him up far above the heaven to the right hand of the glory of the Father: even as God promised by the prophet, saying: *And I will raise up the tabernacle of David that is fallen;*[109] that is, the flesh [110] that was from David. And this our Lord Jesus Christ truly fulfilled, when He gloriously achieved our redemption, that He might truly raise us up, setting us free unto the Father. And if any man will not receive His birth from a virgin, how shall he receive His resurrection from the dead? For it is nothing wonderful and astonishing and extraordinary, if one who was not

born rose from the dead: nay indeed we cannot speak of a resurrection of him who came unto being without birth. For one who is unborn and immortal, and has not undergone birth, will also not undergo death. For he who took not the beginning of man, how could he receive his end?

39. Now, if He was not born, neither did He die; and, if He died not, neither did He rise from the dead; and, if He rose not from the dead, neither did He vanquish death and bring its reign" to nought; and if death be not vanquished, how can we ascend to life, who from the beginning have fallen under death? So then those who take away redemption from man, and believe not in God that He will raise them from the dead, these also despise |105 the birth of our Lord, which He underwent on our behalf, that the Word of God should be made flesh in order that He might manifest the resurrection of the flesh, and might have pre-eminence over all things in the heavens, as the first-born and eldest offspring of the thought of the Father, the Word, fulfilling all things, and Himself guiding and ruling upon earth. For He was the Virgin's first-born, a just and holy man, godfearing, good, well-pleasing to God, perfect in all ways, and delivering from hell all who follow after Him: for He Himself was *the first-begotten of the dead,*[111] the Prince and Author of life unto God.

40. Thus then the Word of God *in all things hath the pre-eminence;*[112] for that He is true man and *Wonderful Counsellor and Mighty God;*[113] calling men anew to fellowship with God, that by fellowship with Him we may partake of incorruption. So then He who was proclaimed by the law through Moses, and by the prophets of the Most High and Almighty God, as Son of the Father of all; He from whom all things are, He who spake with Moses----He came into Judaea, generated from God by the Holy Spirit, and born of the Virgin Mary, even of her who was of the seed of David and of Abraham, Jesus the Anointed of God, |106 showing Himself to be the One who was proclaimed beforehand by the prophets.

41. And His forerunner was John the Baptist) who prepared and made ready the people beforehand for the reception of the Word of life; declaring that He was the Christ, on whom the Spirit of God

rested, mingling with His flesh.[114] His disciples, the witnesses of all His good deeds, and of His teachings and His sufferings and death and resurrection, and of His ascension into heaven after His bodily [115] resurrection----these were the apostles, who after (receiving) the power of the Holy Spirit were sent forth by Him into all the world, and wrought the calling of the Gentiles, showing to mankind the way of life, to turn them from idols and fornication and covetousness, cleansing their souls and bodies by the baptism of water and of the Holy Spirit; which Holy Spirit they had received of the Lord, and they distributed and imparted It to them that believed; and thus they ordered and established the Churches. By faith and love and hope they established that which was foretold by the prophets, the calling of the Gentiles, according to the mercy of God which was extended to them; bringing it to light through the ministration of their service, and admitting them to the promise of the fathers: to wit, that to those who thus believed in and loved the Lord, and continued in holiness and righteousness and patient endurance, the God of all had promised to grant |107 eternal life by the resurrection of the dead; through Him who died and rose again, Jesus Christ, to whom He has delivered over the kingdom of all existing things, and the rule of quick and dead, and also the judgment. And they counselled them by the word of truth to keep their flesh undefiled unto the resurrection and their soul unstained.

42. For such is the state of those who have believed, since in them continually abides the Holy Spirit, who was given by Him in baptism, and is retained by the receiver, if he walks in truth and holiness and righteousness and patient endurance. For this soul has a resurrection in them that believe, the body receiving the soul again, and along with it, by the power of the Holy Spirit, being raised up and entering into the kingdom of God. This is the fruit of the blessing of Japheth, in the calling of the Gentiles, made manifest through the Church, standing in readiness [116] to receive its dwelling in the house of Shem according to the promise of God. That all these things would so come to pass, the Spirit of God declared beforehand by the prophets; that in respect of them the faith of those who worship God in truth should be confirmed. For what was an

impossibility to our nature, and therefore ready to cause incredibility to mankind, this God caused to be made known beforehand by the prophets; in order that, through its having been foretold in times long before, and then at last finding |108 effect in this way, even as it was foretold, we might know that it was God who (thus) proclaimed to us beforehand our redemption.

43. So then we must believe God in all things, for in all things God is true. Now that there was a Son of God, and that He existed not only before He appeared in the world, but also before the world was made, Moses, who was the first that prophesied,[117] says in Hebrew: *Baresith bara Elowin basan benuam samenthares.*[118] And this, translated into our language,[119] is: "The Son in the beginning: God established then the heaven and the earth." [120] This Jeremiah the prophet also testified, saying thus: *Before the morning-star I begat thee: and before the sun (is) thy name;* [121] and that is, before the creation of the world; for together with the world the stars were made. And again the same says: *Blessed is he who was, before he became man:*[122] Because, for God, the Son was (as) the beginning before the creation of the world;[123] but for us (He was) then, when He |109 appeared; and before that He was not for us, who knew Him not.[124] Wherefore also His disciple John, in teaching us who is the Son of God, who was with the Father before the world was made, and that all the things that were made were made by Him, says thus: *In the beginning was the Word, and the Word was with God, and the Word was God, The same was in the beginning with God. All things were made by Him, and without Him was not anything made:*[125] showing with certainty that the Word, who was in the beginning with the Father, and by whom all things were made, this is His Son.

44. And again Moses tells how the Son of God drew near to hold converse with Abraham: *And God appeared unto him by the oak of Mamre in the middle of the day. And looking up with his eyes he beheld, and, lo, three men stood over against him. And he bowed himself down to the earth, and said: Lord, if indeed I have found favour in thy sight.*[126] And all that which follows he spake with the Lord, and the Lord spake with him. Now two of the three were angels; but one was the Son of God, with whom also Abraham spake, pleading on behalf of

the men of Sodom, that they should not perish if at least ten righteous should be found there. And, whilst these were speaking, the two angels entered into Sodom, and Lot received them. And then the Scripture says: *And the Lord rained upon Sodom and Gomorrah brimstone and fire from* |110 *the Lord out of heaven:*[127] that is to say, the Son, who spake with Abraham, being *Lord,* received power to punish the men of Sodom *from the Lord out of heaven,* even from the Father who rules over all. So Abraham was a prophet and saw things to come, which were to take place in human form: even the Son of God, that He should speak with men and eat with them, and then should bring in the judgment from the Father, having received from Him who rules over all the power to punish the men of Sodom.

45. And Jacob, when he went into Mesopotamia, saw Him in a dream, *standing upon the ladder,*[128] that is, the tree, which was set up from earth to heaven; [129] for thereby they that believe on Him go up to the heavens. For His sufferings are our ascension on high. And all such visions point to the Son of God, speaking with men and being in their midst. For it was not the Father of all, who is not seen by the world, the Maker of all who said: *Heaven is my throne, and earth is my footstool: what house will ye build me, or what is the place of my rest?*[130] and who *comprehendeth the earth with his hand, and with his span the heaven* [131]----it was not He that came and stood in a very small space and spake with Abraham; but the Word of God, who was ever with mankind, and made known |111 beforehand what should come to pass in the future, and taught men the things of God.

46. He it is who spake with Moses in the bush, and said: *Seeing have I seen the affliction of thy people that is in Egypt; and I am come down to deliver them.*[132] He it is who came forth and came down for the deliverance of the oppressed, bringing us out from the power of the Egyptians, that is, from all idolatry and impiety; and delivering us from the Red Sea, that is, delivering us from the deadly confusion of the Gentiles and the grievous vexation of their blasphemy. For in them the Word of God prepared and rehearsed beforehand the things concerning us. Then He set forth in types beforehand that which was to be; now in very truth He has brought us out from the cruel service of the Gentiles, and a stream of water in the desert has He made to

flow forth in abundance from a rock; and that rock is Himself; and has given twelve fountains, that is, the teaching of the twelve apostles. And the obstinate unbelievers He brought to an end and consumed in the wilderness; but those who believed on Him, and *in malice were children,* He made to enter into the inheritance of the fathers; whom not Moses, but Jesus puts in possession of the heritage: who also delivers us from Amalek by the expansion of His hands,[133] and brings us to the kingdom of the Father.[134] |112

47. So then the Father is Lord and the Son is Lord, and the Father is God and the Son is God; for that which is begotten of God is God. And so in the substance and power of His being there is shown forth one God; but there is also according to the economy of our redemption both Son and Father. Because to created things the Father of all is invisible and unapproachable,[135] therefore those who are to draw near to God must have their access to the Father through the Son. And yet more plainly and evidently does David speak concerning the Father and the Son as follows: *Thy throne, O God, is for ever and ever: thou hast loved righteousness and hated unrighteousness: therefore God hath anointed thee with the oil of gladness above thy fellows.*[136] For the Son, as being God, receives from the Father, that is, from God, the throne of the everlasting kingdom, and the oil of anointing above His fellows. The oil of anointing is the Spirit, wherewith He has been anointed; and His fellows are prophets and righteous men and apostles, and all who receive the fellowship of His kingdom, that is to say, His disciples.

48. And again David says: *The Lord said unto my Lord: Sit on my right hand, until I make thy* |113 *enemies thy footstool. The rod of thy strength shall the Lord send forth from Sion; and rule thou in the midst of thy enemies. With thee in the beginning in the day of thy power, in the brightness of the holy ones: from the womb before the morning-star I begat thee. The Lord sware and will not repent: Thou art a priest for ever after the order of Melchisedec. And the Lord on thy right hand hath broken in pieces kings in the day of wrath: he shall judge among the Gentiles, he shall fill up the ruins, and shall break in pieces the heads of many on the earth? He shall drink of the brook in the way: therefore shall he lift up the head.* Now hereby he proclaimed that He came into

being before all, and that He rules over the Gentiles and judges all mankind and the kings who now hate Him and persecute His name; for these are His enemies: and in calling Him God's priest for ever, he declared His immortality. And therefore he said: *He shall drink of the brook in the way; therefore shall he lift up the head;* proclaiming the exaltation with glory that followed on His humanity and humiliation and ingloriousness.[137]

49. And again Isaiah the prophet says: *Thus saith the Lord God to my Anointed the Lord,*[138] *whose right hand I have held, that the Gentiles should hearken before him.*[139] And how the Christ is called Son of God and King of the Gentiles, that is, of all |114 mankind; and that He not only is called but is Son of God and King of all, David declares thus: *The Lord said unto me: Thou art my Son, this day have I begotten thee. Ask of me and I will give thee the Gentiles for thy inheritance, and for a possession the utmost parts of the earth.*[140] These things were not said of David; for neither over the Gentiles nor over the utmost parts did he rule, but only over the Jews. So then it is plain that the promise to the Anointed to reign over the utmost parts of the earth is to the Son of God, whom David himself acknowledges as his Lord, saying thus: *The Lord said unto my Lord, Sit on my right hand,*[141] and so forth, as we have said above. For he means that the Father speaks with the Son; as we showed a little before as to Isaiah, that he said thus: *God saith to my Anointed the Lord, that the Gentiles should hearken before him.* For the promise is the same by the two prophets, that He should be King: so that the speech of God is addressed to one and the same, I mean, to Christ the Son of God. Forasmuch as David says: *The Lord said unto me,*[142] it is necessary to say that it is not David who speaks, nor any one of the prophets, in his own person: for it is not a man who speaks the prophecies; but the Spirit of God, assimilating and likening Himself to the persons represented, speaks in the prophets, and utters the words sometimes from Christ and sometimes from the Father.[143] |115

50. So then right fitly Christ says through David that He converses with the Father; and right worthily does He say the other things concerning Himself through the prophets; as in other instances, so also after this manner by Isaiah: *And now thus saith the Lord, who*

formed me as his servant from the womb, to gather Jacob and to gather Israel unto him: and I shall be glorified before the Lord, and my God shall be a strength unto me. And he said; A great thing shall it be to thee to be called my servant, to stablish and confirm the tribe of Jacob, and to turn again the dispersion of Israel: and I have set thee for a light of the Gentiles,[144] *that thou shouldst be for salvation unto the end of the earth.*
[145]

51. Here, first of all, is seen that the Son of God pre-existed, from the fact that the Father spake with Him,[146] and before He was born revealed Him to men: and, next, that He must needs be born a man among men; and that the same God *forms* Him *from the womb*, that is, that of the Spirit of God He should be born; and that He is Lord of all men, and Saviour of them that believe on Him, both Jews and others. For the people of the Jews is called Israel in the Hebrew language, from Jacob their father, who was the first to be called Israel: and Gentiles He calls the whole of mankind. And that the Son of the Father calls Himself *servant,* (this is) on account of His |116 subjection to the Father: for among men also every son is the servant of his father.

52. That Christ, then, being Son of God before all the world, is with the Father; and being with the Father[147] is also nigh and close and joined unto mankind; and is King of all, because the Father has subjected all things unto Him; and Saviour of them that believe on Him----such things do the Scriptures declare. For it is not feasible and possible to enumerate every scripture in order; and from these you may understand the others also which have been spoken in like manner, believing in Christ, and seeking understanding and comprehension from God, so as to understand what has been spoken by the prophets.

53. And that this Christ, who was with the Father, being the Word of the Father, was thereafter to be made flesh and become man and undergo the process of birth and be born of a virgin and dwell among men, the Father of all bringing about His incarnation----Isaiah says thus: *Therefore the Lord himself shall give you a sign: behold, the virgin shall conceive and shall bring forth a son, and ye shall call him*

Emmanuel: butter and honey shall he eat; before he knoweth or selecteth the evil, he chooseth the good: for, before the child knoiveth good or evil, he rejecteth wickedness to choose the good.[148] So he proclaimed His birth from a virgin; and that He was truly man he declared beforehand by His *eating;* and also because he called Him *the* |117 *child;* and further by giving Him a name; for this is the custom also for one that is born. [149] And His name is two-fold: in the Hebrew tongue Messiah Jesus, and in ours Christ Saviour. And the two names are names of works actually wrought. For He was named Christ, because through Him the Father anointed and adorned all things; and because on His coming as man He was anointed with the Spirit of God and His Father. As also by Isaiah He says of Himself: *The Spirit of the Lord is upon me: wherefore he hath anointed me to preach good tidings to the poor.*[150] And (He was named) Saviour for this, that He became the cause of salvation to those who at that time were delivered by Him from all sicknesses and from death,[151] and to those who afterwards believed on Him the author of salvation in the future and for evermore.

54. For this cause then is He Saviour. Now Emmanuel is, being interpreted, *With you God;* [152] or as a yearning cry [153] uttered by the prophet, such as this: *With us shall be God;* according to which it is the explanation and manifestation of the good tidings proclaimed. For *Behold,* H e saith, *the virgin shall conceive and shall bring forth a son;*[154] and He, being God, is to be with us. And, as if altogether astonished [155] at these things, he proclaims in regard to these future events that *With us shall be God.* |118 And yet again concerning His birth the same prophet says in another place: *Before she that travailed gave birth, and before the pains of travail came on, she escaped and was delivered of a man-child.*[156] Thus he showed that His birth from the virgin was unforeseen and unexpected. And again the same prophet says: *Unto us a son is born, and unto us a child is given;*[157] *and his name is called Wonderful Counsellor, Mighty God.*[158]

55. He calls Him *Wonderful Counsellor,* meaning of the Father: whereby it is declared that the Father works all things together with Him; as is contained in the first book of Moses which is entitled Genesis: *And God said, Let us make man after our image and likeness.*

[159] For there is seen in this place the Father speaking to the Son, the Wonderful Counsellor of the Father. Moreover He is also our Counsellor, giving advice; not compelling as God, even though He is *Mighty God,* (as) he says; but giving advice that we should forsake ignorance and acquire knowledge, and |119 depart from error and come to the truth, and put away corruption and receive incorruption.

56. And again Isaiah says: *And they shall wish that they had been burned with fire: for unto us a child is born, and unto us a son is given; whose government is upon his shoulders, and his name is called Angel of great counsel. For I will bring peace upon the riders, again peace and health unto him. Great is his rule, and of his peace there is no bound, upon the throne of David and upon his kingdom, to prosper and complete, to aid and undertake, in righteousness and judgment from this time forth and for evermore.* [160] For hereby the Son of God is proclaimed both as being born and also as eternal King. But *they shall wish that they had been burned with fire* (is said) of those who believe not on Him, and who have done to Him all that they have done: for they shall say in the judgment, How much better that we had been burned with fire before the Son of God was born, than that, when He was born, we should not have believed on Him. Because for those who died before Christ appeared there is hope that in the judgment of the risen [161] they may obtain salvation, even such as feared God and died in righteousness and had in them the Spirit of God, as the patriarchs and prophets and righteous men. But for those who after Christ's appearing believed not on Him, there is a vengeance without pardon in the judgment. |120Now in this: *Whose government is upon his shoulder,* the cross is in a figure declared, on which He was nailed back. For that which was and is a reproach to Him, and for His sake to us, even the cross, this same is, says he, His *government,* being a sign of His kingdom. And, *Angel of great counsel,* he says; that is, of the Father whom He hath declared unto us.

57. That the Son of God should be born, and in what way He was to be born, and that He should be shown to be Christ----from what has been said it is plain how this was made known beforehand by the prophets. And in addition to this, in what land and among whom of mankind He was to be born and to appear, this also was proclaimed

beforehand with words such as these. Moses in Genesis says thus: *There shall not fail a prince from Judah, nor a leader from his loins, until he shall come for whom it remaineth; and he shall be the expectation of the Gentiles: washing his robe in wine, and his garment in the blood of the grape.*[162] Now Judah was the ancestor of the Jews, the son of Jacob; from whom also they obtained the name. |121 And there failed not a prince among them and a leader, until the coming of Christ. But from the time of His coming the might of the quiver was captured,[163] the land of the Jews was given over into subjection to the Romans, and they had no longer a prince or king of their own. For He was come, *for whom remaineth* in heaven the kingdom; who also *washed his robe in wine, and his garment in the blood of the grape.* His robe as also His garment are those who believe on Him, whom also He cleansed, redeeming us by His blood. And His blood is said to be *blood of the grape:* for even as the blood of the grape no man maketh, but God produceth, and *maketh glad* them that drink thereof, so also His flesh and blood no man wrought, but God made. *The Lord Himself gave the sign* of the virgin, even that Emmanuel which was from the virgin; who also *maketh glad* them that drink of Him, that is to say, who receive His Spirit, (even) *everlasting gladness.* Wherefore also He is *the expectation of the Gentiles,* of those who *hope in Him;* because we expect of Him that He will establish again the kingdom. 164

58. And again Moses says: *There shall rise a star out of Jacob; and a leader* [165] *shall be raised up out of Israel;* showing yet more plainly that the |122 dispensation of His coming in flesh should be among the Jews. And from Jacob and from the tribe of Judah He who was born, coming down from heaven, took upon Him this economy of dispensation: for the *star* appeared in heaven. And by *leader* he means king, because He is the King of all the redeemed. And at His birth the star appeared to the Magi who dwelt in the east;[166] and thereby they learned that Christ was born; and they came to Judaea, led by the star; until the star came to Bethlehem where Christ was born, and entered the house wherein was laid the child, wrapped in swaddling-clothes; and it stood over His head,[167] declaring to the Magi the Son of God, the Christ.

59. Moreover Isaiah himself yet further says: *A nd there shall come forth a rod out of the roots of Jesse, and a flower from his root shall come forth. And the spirit of God shall rest upon him; the spirit of wisdom and of understanding, the spirit of counsel and of might, the spirit of knowledge and of godliness: the spirit of the fear of God shall fill him? Not according to opinion shall he judge, and not according to speech shall he reprove: but he shall judge judgment for the humble, and shew mercy to the humble of the earth. And he shall smite the earth with the word of his mouth, and with the |123 breath of his lips* [168] *shall he slay the impious man. And he shall be girt about his loins with righteousness, and with truth encompassed about his reins. And the wolf shall feed with the lamb, and the leopard with the kid, and the calf and the lion shall pasture together. And a sucking child shall put his hand on the hole of the asps, and on the lair of the offspring of the asps, and they shall not hurt him. And in that day there shall be a root of Jesse, and he that riseth up to rule the Gentiles: in him shall the Gentiles hope: and his rising up shall be honour.* [169] By these words he states that He was born from her who was of the race of David and of Abraham. For Jesse was the descendant of Abraham, and the father of David; (and David's) descendant the virgin was who conceived Christ. Now (as to) the *rod:* for this cause also Moses with[170] a rod showed the mighty works to Pharaoh: and with other men also the rod is a sign of rule. And by *flower* he means His flesh; [171] for from spirit it budded forth, as we have said before.

60. Now, *Not according to opinion shall he judge, and not according to speech shall he reprove: but he shall judge judgment for the humble, and shall show mercy to the humble on the earth*----(by this) he the |124 more establishes and declares His godhead. For to judge without respect of persons and partiality, and not as favouring the illustrious, but affording to the humble worthy and like and equal treatment, accords with the height and summit of the righteousness of God: for God is influenced and moved by none, save only the righteous. And to show mercy is the peculiar attribute of God, who by mercy is able to save. And *He shall smite the earth with a word,* and *slay the impious* with a word only: this belongs to God who worketh all things with a word. And in saying: *He shall be girt about his loins with righteousness,*

and with truth encompassed about his reins, he declares His human form and aspect, and His own surpassing righteousness.

61. Now as to the union and concord and peace of the animals of different kinds,[172] which by nature are opposed and hostile to each other, the Elders say that so it will be in truth at the coming of Christ, when He is to reign over all. For already in a symbol he announces the gathering together in peace and concord, through the name of Christ, of men of unlike races and (yet) of like dispositions. For, when thus united, on the righteous, who are likened to calves and lambs and kids and sucking |125 children, those inflict no hurt at all who in the former time were, through their rapacity, like wild beasts in manners and disposition, both men and women; so much so that some of them were like wolves and lions, ravaging the weaker and warring on their equals; while the women (were like) leopards or asps, who slew, it may be, even their loved ones with deadly poisons, or by reason of lustful desire. (But now) coming together in one name [173] they have acquired righteous habits by the grace of God, changing their wild and untamed nature. And this has come to pass already. For those who were before exceeding wicked, so that they left no work of ungodliness undone, learning of Christ and believing on Him, have at once believed and been changed, so as to leave no excellenpy of righteousness undone; so great is the transformation which faith in Christ the Son of God effects for those who believe on Him. And he says: *Rising up to rule the Gentiles,* because He is to die and rise again, and be confessed and believed as the Son of God (and) King. On this account he says: *And His rising up shall be honour:* that is, glory; for then was He glorified as God, when He rose.

62. Wherefore again the prophet says:[174] *In that day I will raise up the tabernacle of David that is fallen:*[175] that body [176] of Christ, which, as we have said before, is born of David, he plainly declares as after death rising from the dead. For the body is called a |126 tabernacle. [177] For by these words he says that He who according to the flesh is of the race of David will be Christ the Son of God; and that He will die and rise again, and that He is in aspect a man, but in power God; and that He Himself will be as judge of all the world and as the only

worker of righteousness and redeemer----all this the Scripture declared.

63. And again the prophet Micah speaks of the place where Christ should be born, that it should be in Bethlehem of Judaea, saying thus: *And thou, Bethlehem of Judaea, art thou the least among the princes of Judah? for out of thee shall come a prince who shall feed my people Israel.* [178] But Bethlehem is the native place of David: so that not only in respect of the Virgin who bore Him is He of David's race, but also in respect of His birth in Bethlehem the native place of David.

64. And again David says that of his race Christ is to be born, (speaking) after this manner: *For David my [179] servant's sake turn not away the face of thy Christ. The Lord sware truth unto David, and he will not disappoint him: Of the fruit of thy body* |127 *will I set on thy throne: if thy children shall keep my covenant and my testimonies, which I covenanted with them, their sons for evermore (shall sit upon thy throne).* [180] But none of the sons of David reigned for evermore, nor was their kingdom for evermore; for it was brought to nought. But the king that was born of David, He is Christ. All these testimonies declare in plain terms His descent according to the flesh, and the race and place where He was to be born; so that no man should seek among the Gentiles or elsewhere for the birth of the Son of God, but in Bethlehem of Judaea from Abraham and from David's race.

65. And the manner of His entry into Jerusalem, which was the capital of Judaea, where also was His royal seat and the temple of God, the prophet Isaiah declares: *Say ye to the daughter of Sion, Behold a king cometh unto thee, meek and sitting upon an ass, a colt the foal of an ass.* [181] For, sitting on an ass's colt, so He entered into Jerusalem, the multitudes strewing and putting down for Him their garments. And by *the daughter of Sion* he means Jerusalem.

66. So then, that the Son of God should be born, and in what manner born, and where He was to be born, and that Christ is the one eternal King, [182] the prophets thus declared. And again they told beforehand concerning Him how, sprung from mankind, He should heal those whom He healed, |128 and raise the dead whom He raised,

and be hated and despised and undergo sufferings and be put to death and crucified, even as He was hated and despised and put to death.

67. At this point let us speak of His healings. Isaiah says thus: *He took our infirmities and bare our sicknesses:*[183] that is to say, He shall take, and shall bear. For there are passages in which the Spirit of God through the prophets recounts things that are to be as having taken place. For that which with God is essayed and conceived of as determined to take place, is reckoned as having already taken place: and the Spirit, regarding and seeing the time in which the issues of the prophecy are fulfilled, utters the words (accordingly). And concerning the kind of healing, thus will He make mention, saying: *In that day shall the deaf hear the words of the book, and in darkness and in mist the eyes of the blind shall see.*[184] And the same says again: *Be strong, ye weak hands and feeble and trembling knees: be comforted, ye that are of a fearful mind. Be strong, fear not. Behold, our God will recompense judgment: He will come and save us. Then shall the eyes of the blind be opened, and the ears of the deaf shall hear: then shall the lame man leap as an hart, and the tongue of the stammerers shall be plain.*[185] And concerning the dead, that they shall be raised, he says thus: *The dead shall be raised, and they that are in the tombs* |129 *shall be raised.* [186] And in bringing these things to pass He shall be believed to be the Son of God.

68. And that He shall be despised and tormented and in the end put to death, Isaiah says thus: *Behold, my son shall understand,*[187] *and shall be exalted and glorified greatly. Even as many shall be astonished at thee, so without glory shall thy form be from men. And many races shall be astonished, and kings shall shut their mouths: for they to whom it was not declared concerning him shall see, and they who have not heard shall consider. Lord, who hath believed our report? and to whom hath the arm of the Lord been revealed? We declared before him as a child, as a root in a dry ground: and there is to him no form nor glory: and we saw him, and he had no form nor beauty: and his form was without honour, meaner than that of other men: a man in chastisement, and acquainted with the bearing of pain; for his face was turned away, he was dishonoured and made of no account. He beareth our sins, and for our*

sakes endureth pain: and we accounted him to be in pain and chastisement and affliction. But he was wounded for our iniquities, and was tormented for our sins. The discipline of our peace (was) upon him; by his stripes we were healed.[188] By these words it is declared that He was tormented; as also David says: And I was tormented.[189] Now |130 David was never tormented, but Christ (was), when the command was given that He should be crucified. And again by Isaiah His Word says: I gave my back to scourging, and my cheeks to smiting: and my face I turned not away from the shame of spitting.[190] And Jeremiah the prophet says the same, thus: He shall give his cheek to the smiter: he shall be filled with reproaches.[191] All these things Christ suffered.

69. Now what follows in Isaiah is this: By his stripes we were healed. All we like sheep went astray: a man in his way went astray: and the Lord delivered him up to our sins.[192] It is manifest therefore that by the will of the Father these things occurred to Him for the sake of our salvation. Then he says: And he by reason of his suffering opened not (his) mouth: as a sheep to the slaughter was he brought, as a lamb [193] dumb before the shearer.[194] Behold how he declares His voluntary coming to death. And when the prophet says: In the humiliation his judgment was taken away, he signifies the appearance of His humiliation: according to the form of the abasement was the taking away of judgment. And the taking away of judgment is for some unto salvation, and to some unto the torments of perdition. For there is a taking away for a person, and also from a person. |131 So also with the judgment----those for whom it is taken away have it unto the torments of their perdition: but those from whom it is taken away are saved by it. Now those took away to themselves the judgment who crucified Him, and when they had done this to Him believed not on Him: for through that judgment which was taken away by them they shall be destroyed with torments. And from them that believe on Him the judgment is taken away, and they are no longer under it. And the judgment is that which by fire will be the destruction of the unbelievers at the end of the world.

70. Then he says: His generation who shall declare?[195] This was said to warn us, lest on account of His enemies and the outrage of His sufferings we should despise Him as a mean and contemptible man.

For He who endured all this has an un-declarable generation; for by generation He means descent; (for) He who is His Father is undeclarable and unspeakable. Know therefore that such descent was His who endured these sufferings; and despise Him not because of the sufferings which for thy sake He of purpose endured, but fear Him because of His descent.

71. And in another place Jeremiah says: *The Spirit of our face, the Lord Christ;*[196] and how He *was taken in their snares, of whom, we said, Under his shadow we shall live among the Gentiles.* That, being (the) Spirit of God, Christ was to become a |132 suffering man the Scripture declares; and is, as it were, amazed and astonished at His sufferings, that in such manner He was to endure sufferings, *under whose shadow we said that we should live.* And by *shadow* he means His body.[197] For just as a shadow is made by a body, so also Christ's body was made by His Spirit.[198] But, further, the humiliation and contemptibility of His body he indicates by the shadow. For, as the shadow of bodies standing upright is upon the ground and is trodden upon, so also the body of Christ fell upon the ground by His sufferings and was trodden on indeed. And he named Christ's body a shadow, because the Spirit overshadowed it, as it were, with glory and covered it.[199] Moreover oftentimes when the Lord .passed by, they laid those who were held by divers diseases in the way, and on whomsoever His shadow fell, they were healed.[200]

72. And again the same prophet (says) thus concerning the sufferings of Christ: *Behold how the righteous is destroyed, and no man layeth it to heart; and righteous men are taken away, and no man understandeth. For from the face of iniquity is the taking away of the righteous: peace shall be his burial, he hath been taken away from the midst.*[201] And who else is perfectly righteous, but the Son of God, who makes righteous and perfects them that believe on Him, who like unto Him are persecuted |133 and put to death? [202] But in saying: *Peace shall be his burial,* he declares how on account of our redemption He died: for it is in the peace of redemption: and (also he declares) that by His death those who aforetime were enemies and opposed to one another, believing with one accord upon Him, should have peace with one another, becoming friends and beloved on account of their common

faith in Him; as indeed they have become. But in saying: *He hath been taken away from the midst,* he signifies His resurrection from the dead. Moreover because He appeared no more after His death and burial, the prophet declares that after dying and rising again He was to remain immortal, (saying) thus: *He asked life, and thou gavest (if) him, and length of days for ever and ever.*[203] Now what is this that he says, *He asked life,* since He was about to die? He proclaims His resurrection from the dead, and that being raised from the dead He is immortal. For He received both *life,* that He should rise, and *length of days for ever and ever,* that He should be incorruptible.

73. And again David says thus concerning the death and resurrection of Christ: *I laid me down and slept: I awaked, for the Lord received me.* [204] David said not this of himself, for he was not raised after death: but the Spirit of Christ, who (spake) also in other prophets concerning Him, says here by David: *I laid me down and slept: I* |134 *awaked, for the Lord received me.* By sleep he means death; for He arose again.

74. And again David (says) thus concerning the sufferings of Christ: *Why did the Gentiles rage, and the people imagine vain things? Kings rose up on the earth, and princes were gathered together, against the Lord and his Anointed.*[205] For Herod the king of the Jews and Pontius Pilate, the governor of Claudius Caesar,[206] came together and condemned Him to be crucified.[207] For Herod feared, as though He were to be an earthly king, lest he should be expelled by Him from the kingdom. But Pilate was constrained by Herod and the Jews that were with him against his will to deliver Him to death: (for they threatened him) if he should not rather do this[208] than act contrary to Caesar, by letting go a man who was called a king.

75. And further concerning the sufferings of Christ the same prophet says: *Thou hast repelled and despised us; and hast cast away thine Anointed. Thou hast broken the covenant of my*[209] *servant; thou hast cast his holiness to the ground. Thou hast overthrown all his hedges; thou hast made his* |135 *strongholds to tremble.*[210] *They that pass on the way have ravaged him; he is becdme a reproach to his neighbours. Thou hast exalted the right hand of his oppressors; thou hast made his enemies to rejoice over*

him, *Thou hast turned away the help of his sword, and gavest him not a hand in the battle. Thou hast removed and thrown him down from purification; thou hast overturned his throne upon the ground. Thou hast shortened the days of his time, and hast poured forth shame upon him.* That He should endure these things, and that too by the will of the Father, he manifestly declared: for by the will of the Father He was to endure sufferings.

76. And Zechariah says thus: *Sword, awake against my shepherd, and against the man (that is) my companion. Smite* [211] *the shepherd, and the sheep of the flock shall be scattered.*[212] And this came to pass when He was taken by the Jews: for all the disciples forsook Him, fearing lest they should die with Him. For not yet did they stedfastly believe on Him, until they had seen Him risen from the dead.

77. Again He says in the Twelve Prophets:[213] *And they bound him and brought him as a present to the king.*[214] For Pontius Pilate was governor of Judaea, and he had at that time resentful enmity against Herod the king of the Jews.[215] But then, when Christ was brought to him bound, Pilate sent |136 Him to Herod, giving command to enquire of him, that he might know of a certainty what he should desire concerning Him; making Christ a convenient occasion of reconciliation with the king.

78. And in Jeremiah He thus declares His death and descent into hell, saying: *And the Lord the Holy One of Israel, remembered his dead, which aforetime fell asleep in the dust of the earth; and he went down unto them, to bring the tidings of his salvation, to deliver them.*[216] In this place He also renders the cause of His death: for His descent into hell was the salvation of them that had passed away.

79. And, again, concerning His cross Isaiah says thus: *I have stretched out my hands all the day long to a disobedient and gainsaying people.*[217] For this is an indication of the cross,[218] And yet more manifestly David says: *Hunting-dogs encompassed me: the assembly of evil-doers came about me. They pierced my hands and my feet.*[219] And again he says: *My heart became even as wax melting in the midst* |137 *of my body; and they put asunder my bones,* and again he says: *Spare my soul*

from the sword and nail my flesh: for the assembly of evil-doers hath risen up against me.[220] In these words with manifest clearness he signifies that He should be crucified. And Moses says this same thing to the people, thus: *And thy life shall be hanged up before thine eyes, and thou shalt fear by day and by night, and thou shalt not believe in thy life.*[221]

80. And again David says: *They looked upon me, they parted my garments among them, and upon my vesture they cast lots.*[222] For at His crucifixion the soldiers parted His garments as they were wont; and the garments they parted by tearing; but for the vesture, because it was woven from the top and was not sewn, they cast lots, that to whomsoever it should fall he should take it.[223]

81. And again Jeremiah the prophet says: *And they took the thirty pieces of silver, the price of him that was sold, whom they bought from the children of Israel; and they gave them for the potter's field, as the Lord commanded me.*[224] For Judas, being one of Christ's disciples, agreed with the Jews and covenanted with them, when he saw they desired to kill Him, because he had been reproved by Him: and he took the thirty *staters* [226] of the province, and betrayed Christ unto them[225]: and then, repenting of |138 what he had done, he gave the silver back again to the rulers of the Jews, and hanged himself. But they, thinking it not right to cast it into their treasury, because it was the price of blood, bought with it the ground that was a certain potter's for the burial of strangers.

82. And at His crucifixion, when He asked a drink, they gave Him to drink vinegar mingled with gall.[227] And this was declared through David: *They gave gall to my meat, and in my thirst they gave me vinegar to drink.*[228]

83. And that, being raised from the dead, He was to ascend into heaven, David says thus: *The chariot of God (is) ten-thousandfold, thousands are the drivers: the Lord (is) among them in Sinai in (his) sanctuary.*[229] *He ascended up on high, he led captivity captive: he received, he gave gifts to men.*[230] And by *captivity* he means the destruction of the rule of the apostate angels. He declares also the place where He was to ascend into heaven from the earth. For *the*

Lord, he says, *from Sion ascended up on high.* For over against Jerusalem, |139 on the mount which is called (the Mount) of Olives, after He was risen from the dead, He assembled His disciples, and expounded to them the things concerning the kingdom of heaven; and they saw that He ascended, and they saw how the heavens were opened and received Him.

84. And the same says David again: *Lift up your gates, ye rulers; and be ye lift up, ye everlasting gates, and the King of glory shall come in.*[231] For the everlasting gates are the heavens. But because the Word descended invisible to created things, He was not made known in His descent to them. Because the Word was made flesh, He was visible in His ascension; and, when the powers saw Him, the angels below cried out to those who were on the firmament: *Lift up your gates; and be ye lift up, ye everlasting gates, that the King of glory may come in.* And when they marvelled and said: *Who is this?* those who had already seen Him testified a second time: *The Lord strong and mighty, he is the King of glory.*[232]

85. And being raised from the dead and exalted at the Father's right hand, He awaits the time appointed by the Father for the judgment, when all enemies shall be put under Him. Now the enemies are all those who were found in apostasy, angels and archangels and powers and thrones, who despised the truth. And the prophet David |140 himself says thus: *The Lord said unto my Lord, Sit on my right hand, until I make thine enemies thy footstool.*[233] And that He ascended thither, whence He had come down, David says: *From the end of heaven is his going forth, and his cessation even at the end of heaven.* Then he signifies his judgment: *And there is none that shall be hid from his heat.*[234]

86. If then the prophets prophesied that the Son of God was to appear upon the earth, and prophesied also where on the earth and how and in what manner He should make known His appearance, and all these prophecies the Lord took upon Himself; our faith in Him was well-founded, and the tradition of the preaching (is) true: that is to say, the testimony of the apostles, who being sent forth by the Lord preached in all the world the Son of God, who came to

suffer, and endured to the destruction of death and the quickening of the flesh: that by the putting away of the enmity towards God, which is unrighteousness, we should obtain peace with Him, doing that which is pleasing to Him. And this was declared by the prophets in the words: *How beautiful are the feet of them that bring tidings of peace, and of them that bring tidings of good things.*[235] And that these were to go forth from Judaea and from Jerusalem, to declare to us *the word* of God, which is *the law* for us, Isaiah says thus: *For from Sion shall come* |141 *forth the law, and the word of the Lord from Jerusalem.*[236] And that in all the earth they were to preach, David says: *Into all the earth went forth their speech, and their words to the ends of the world.*[237]

87. And that not by the much-speaking of the law, but by the brevity of faith and love,[238] men were to be saved, Isaiah says thus: *A word brief and short in righteousness: for a short word will God make in the whole world.*[239] And therefore the apostle Paul says: *Love is the fulfilling of the law:*[240] for he who loves God has fulfilled the law. Moreover the Lord, when He was asked which is the first commandment, said: *Thou shalt love the Lord thy God with all thy heart and with all thy strength.*[1] *And the second is like unto it: Thou shalt love thy neighbour as thyself. On these two commandments,* He says, *all the law hangeth and the prophets.*[241] So then by our faith in Him He has made our love to God and our neighbour to grow, making us godly and righteous and good. And therefore *a short word* has God made on the earth *in the world.*

88. And that after His ascension He was to be exalted above all, and that there shall be none to be compared and equalled unto Him, Isaiah says thus:[2] *Who is he that entereth into judgment (with me)? Let him stand up against (me). And* |142 *who is he who is justified? Let him draw near to the Lords Son. Woe unto you, for ye shall grow old as a garment, and the moth shall devour you. And all flesh shall be humbled and abased, and the Lord alone shall be exalted in the highest.*[242] And that in the end by His name they should be saved who served God, Isaiah says: *And on those who serve me a new name shall be called, which shall be blessed upon the earth: and they shall bless the true God.* [243] And that this blessing He Himself should bring about, and Himself should redeem us by His own blood, Isaiah declared, saying:

No mediator, no angel, but the Lord himself saved them; because he loved them and spared them: he himself redeemed them.[244]

89. That He would not send back the redeemed to the legislation of Moses----for the law was fulfilled in Christ----but would have them live [245] in newness by the Word, through faith in the Son of God and love, Isaiah declared, saying: *Remember not the former things, nor bring to mind the things that were in the beginning. Behold I make new (things), which shall now spring up, and ye shall know (them). And I will make in the wilderness a way, and in the waterless place streams, to give drink to my chosen race, and to my people whom I have purchased to declare my virtues.*[246] Now a *wilderness* and a *waterless place* was at first the calling of the Gentiles: for the Word had not passed through |143 them, nor given them the Holy Spirit to drink; who fashioned the new *way* of godliness and righteousness, and made copious *streams* to spring forth, disseminating over the earth the Holy Spirit; even as it had been promised through the prophets, that in the end of the days He should pour out the Spirit upon the face of the earth.

90. Therefore *by newness of the spirit* is our calling, and not *in the oldness of the letter;*[247] even as Jeremiah prophesied: *Behold the days come, saith the Lord, that I will accomplish for the house of Israel and for the house of Judah the covenant of the testament which I covenanted with their fathers, in the day when I took them by the hand to lead them out of the land of Egypt: because they continued not in the covenant, and I regarded them not, saith the Lord. For this is the covenant of the testament that I will covenant with the house of Israel after those days, saith the Lord: I will put my laws [248] into their minds, and write them in their hearts; and I will be to them a God, and they shall be to me a people: and they shall not teach any more every man his neighbour, and every man his brother, saying, Know the Lord: for all shall |144 know me, from the least to the greatest of them. For I will pardon and be merciful unto the sins of their iniquities, and their sins will I remember no more.*[249]

91. And that these promises the calling from among the Gentiles should inherit, to whom also the new testament was opened up, Isaiah says thus: *These things saith the God of Israel: In that day a man*

shall trust[250] *in his Maker, and his eyes shall look to the Holy One of Israel: and they shall not trust in altars, nor in the work of their own hands, which their fingers have made.*[251] For very plainly this was said of such as have forsaken idols and believed in God our Maker through the Holy One of Israel. And the Holy One of Israel is Christ: and He became visible to men, and to Him we look eagerly and behold Him; and we trust not in altars, nor in the works of our hands.

92. And that He should become visible [252] amongst us----for the Son of God became Son of man----and be found of us who before had no knowledge (of Him), the Word Himself says thus in Isaiah: *I became manifest to them that sought me not; I was found of them that asked not for me. I said, Behold, here am I, to a race that called not on my name.* [253]

93. And that this race was to become an holy people was declared in the Twelve Prophets by Hosea, thus: *I will call that which was not (my)* |145 *people, my people; and her that was not beloved, beloved. It shall come to pass that in the place where it was called not my people, there shall they be called sons of the Living God.*[254] This also is that which was said by John the Baptist: *That God is able of these stones to raise up sons to Abraham.*[255] For our hearts being withdrawn and taken away from the stony worship by means of faith behold God, and become sons of Abraham, who was justified by faith. And therefore God says by Ezekiel the prophet: *And I will give them another heart, and a new spirit will I give them: and I will withdraw and take away the stony heart from their flesh, and I will give them another heart of flesh: so that they shall walk in my precepts, and shall keep my ordinances and do them. And they shall be to me for a people, and I will be to them for a God.* [256]

94. So then by the new calling a change of hearts in the Gentiles came to pass through the Word of God, when *He was made flesh and tabernacled* with men; as also His disciple John says: *And his Word was made flesh and dwelt among us.*[257] Wherefore the Church beareth much fruit of the redeemed: because no longer Moses (as) mediator nor Elijah (as) messenger, but the Lord Himself has redeemed us,

granting many more children to the Church than to the first Synagogue;[258] |146 as Isaiah declared, saying: *Rejoice thou barren, that didst not bear.*[259] The *barren* is the Church, which never at all in former times presented sons to God. *Cry out and call, thou that didst not travail: for the children of the desolate are more than of her which hath an husband.* Now the first Synagogue had as husband the Law.

95. Moreover Moses in Deuteronomy says that the Gentiles should be *the head,* and the unbelieving people *the tail.* And again he says: *Ye provoked me to jealousy with those that are no gods, and angered me with your idols: and I will provoke you to jealousy with that which is no nation, and with a foolish nation will I anger you.*[260] Because they forsook the God who is, and worshipped and served the gods who are not; and they slew the prophets of God, and *prophesied for Baal,*[261] who was the idol of the Canaanites. And the Son of God, who is,[262] they despised and condemned, but they chose Barabbas the robber who had been taken for murder: and the eternal King [263] they disavowed, and they acknowledged as their king the temporal Caesar. (So) it pleased God to grant their inheritance to the foolish Gentiles, even to those who were not of the polity of God and knew not what God is. Since, then, by this calling life has been given (us), and God has summed up again for Himself in us the faith of Abraham, we ought |147 not to turn back any more----I mean, to the first legislation. For we have received the Lord of the Law, the Son of God; and by faith in Him we learn to love God with all our heart, and our neighbour as ourselves. Now the love of God is far from all sin,[264] and love to the neighbour worketh no ill to the neighbour.[265]

96. Wherefore also we need not the Law as a tutor. Behold, with the Father we speak, and in His presence we stand, being *children in malice,* and grown strong in all righteousness and soberness.[266] For no longer shall the Law say, *Do not commit adultery,* to him who has no desire at all for another's wife; and *Thou shalt not kill,* to him who has put away from himself all anger and enmity; (and) *Thou shalt not covet thy neighbour s field or ox or ass,*[267] to those who have no care at all for earthly things, but store up the heavenly fruits: nor *An eye for an eye, and a tooth for a tooth,*[268] to him who counts no man his enemy, but all men his neighbours, and therefore cannot stretch out his hand at

all for vengeance. It will not require tithes of him who consecrates all his possessions to God, leaving father and mother and all his kindred, and following the Word of God. And there will be no command to remain idle for one day of rest, to him who perpetually keeps sabbath, [269] that is to |148 say, who in the temple of God, which is man's body, does service to God, and in every hour works righteousness. *For I desire mercy,* He saith, *and not sacrifice; and the knowledge of God more than burnt offerings. But the wicked that sacrificeth to me a calf is as if he should kill a dog; and that offereth fine flour, as though (he offered] swine's blood. But whosoever shall call on the name of the Lord shall be saved.* And there is *none other name* of the Lord *given under heaven whereby men are saved,*[270] save that of God, which is Jesus Christ the Son of God, to which also the demons are subject and evil spirits and all apostate energies, by the invocation of the name of Jesus Christ, crucified under Pontius Pilate.[271]

97. He is separated and withdrawn from among men, and (yet) there is a separation and division among mankind; and wheresoever any of those who believe on Him shall invoke and call upon Him and do His will, He is near and present, fulfilling the requests of those who with pure hearts call upon Him. Whereby receiving salvation, we continually give thanks to God, who by His great, inscrutable and unsearchable wisdom delivered us, and proclaimed the salvation from heaven ---- to wit, the visible coming of our Lord, that is, His living as man ----to which we by ourselves could not attain: for *the things which are impossible with men are possible with God.*[272] Wherefore also Jeremiah saith concerning her *(i. e.* wisdom):[273] *Who hath gone up into* |149 *heaven, and taken her, and brought her down from the clouds? Who hath gone over the sea, found her, and will bring her for choice gold? There is none that hath found her way, nor any that comprehendeth her path. But he that knoweth all things knoweth her by his understanding: he that prepareth the earth for evermore, hath filled it with four-footed beasts: he that sendeth forth the light and it goeth; he called it, and it obeyed him with fear: and the stars shined in their watches, and were glad: he called them, and they said Here we be; they shined with gladness unto him that made them. This is our God: there shall none other be accounted of in comparison with him. He hath found out every way by*

knowledge, and hath given it unto Jacob his servant, and to Israel that is beloved of him. Afterward did he appear upon earth, and was conversant with men. This is the book of the commandments of God, and of the law which endureth for ever. All they that hold it fast (are appointed) to life: but such as leave it shall die. Now by *Jacob* and *Israel* he means the Son of God, who received power from the Father over our life, and after having received this brought it down to us who were far off from Him, when He *appeared on earth and was conversant with men,* mingling and mixing the Spirit of God the |150 Father with the creature formed by God,[274] that man might be *after the image and likeness* of God.

98. This, beloved, is the preaching of the truth, and this is the manner of our redemption, and this is the way of life, which the prophets proclaimed, and Christ established, and the apostles delivered, and the Church in all the world hands on to her children. This must we keep with all certainty, with a sound will and pleasing to God, with good works and right-willed disposition.

99. So that none should imagine God the Father to be other than our Creator, as the heretics imagine; (for) they despise the God who is, and make gods of that which is not; and they fashion a Father of their own above our Creator, and imagine that they have found out for themselves something greater than the truth. For all these are impious and blasphemers against their Creator and against the Father, as we have shown in the *Exposure and Overthrow of Knowledge falsely so-called.* And others again reject the coming of the Son of God and the dispensation of His incarnation, which the apostles delivered and the prophets declared beforehand, even such as should be the summing up of mankind, as we have shown you in brief: and such also are reckoned amongst those who are lacking in faith. And others receive not the gifts of the Holy Spirit, and cast away from |151 themselves the prophetic grace, watered whereby man bears the fruit of life unto God: and these are they of whom Isaiah speaks: *For they shall be,* saith he, *as an oak that is stripped of leaves, and as a garden that hath no water.*[275] And such are in no wise serviceable to God, seeing that they cannot bear any fruit.

100. So then in respect of the three points[276] of our seal error has strayed widely from the truth. For either they reject the Father, or they accept not the Son and speak against the dispensation of His incarnation; or else they receive not the Spirit, that is, they reject prophecy. And of all such must we beware, and shun their ways, if in very truth we desire to be well-pleasing to God and to attain the redemption that is from Him.

Notes:

[Selected footnotes moved to the end and renumbered.]

1. [1] This opening section is in the manner of the introductions to each of the five books *Against Heresies:* in the first of these, of which the Greek is preserved, we have parallels to language used here: ...

2. [2] "To shew forth the preaching." This corresponds to the wording of the title: the e0pi/deicij, *ostensio,* or "demonstration" of the Apostolic Preaching.

3. [3] Lit. "a more essential remembrancer."

4. [2] Or, "spirit." The Armenian word for "spirit" (pneu~ma) is sometimes used also for "soul " (yuxh&): the context shows that it is so used here.

5. [1] Lit. "I am the Existing One,"as in LXX .... In III, vi. 2 the words are quoted as spoken by the Father.

6. [2] Here, as usual, the LXX is followed...

7. [3] Cf. I, i. 20:.... The Arm. has taken over the Greek word kanw&n.

8. Ps. i. 1.

9. Ex. iii. 14.

10. Isa. vii. 9

11. ² This passage is obscure, and I cannot feel any confidence in my rendering of it. The Armenian translator has probably misunderstood the construction of the Greek: his verbs are all in the infinitive, which suggests that Irenaeus is recording what the faith teaches. The words "made God" represent qeopoiei=sqai. This word, if not traceable elsewhere in Irenaeus, is found in other early writers: *e. g.* Hippolytus, *Philos.* x. 34: .... It is frequent in Athanasius; *e. g. De Incarn.* 54: .... In Irenaeus the thought finds expression in various forms: see IV, lxiii. 3: "quoniam non ab initio dii facti sumus, sed primo quidem homines, tunc demum dii:" also III, vi. i.

12. ¹ This is a reminiscence of controversy with the heretics who denied that the Good God of the New Testament was the Creator God of the Old Testament: see IV, xxxiv. 2: "non enim aliena sed sua tradidit ei" (of the Father committing all things to the Son); V, ii. i: "vani autem qui in aliena dicunt Dominum venisse, velut aliena concupiscentem" (where the Arm. enables us to correct the Latin, which has "Deum ").

13. ² In IV, xxxiv. 2 he quotes, as "Scripture," the Shepherd of Hermas, *Mand.* I: .... Cf. also I, XV. 1.

14. ⁴ Or "shown to be": cf. V, xviii. 1: "Et sic unus Deus Pater ostenditur (= dei/knutai)."

15. Cf. Isa. xliii. 10.

16. ¹ God is logiko&j, therefore by lo&goj He created the world. The play on the words is given by the Armenian, but cannot be given by the English translation.

17. Ps. xxxiii. 6.

18. ² "Gives body:" apparently representing swmatopoiei=: cf. I. i. 9, of the Demiurge of Valentinus: ....

19. Eph. iv. 6.

20. Cf. Gal. iv. 6.

21. ¹ Lit. "head:" cf. cc. 7, 100.

22. ² This is fully worked out in IV, lv. 1-6: the prophets were "members of Christ," and so each, according to the "member" that he was, declared his portion of prophecy, all together announcing the whole.

23. ³ The same double rendering of a0nakefalaiw&sasqai (Eph. i. 10) is found in the Arm. version of V, i. 2.

24. ⁴ IV, xi. 4: "visibilem et palpabilem;" cf. IV, xiii. 1, where the Arm. shows that the Latin "passibilis" should be corrected to "palpabilis."

25. Rom. ii. 4-6.

26. ¹ An account of the late Jewish teaching as to the Seven Heavens is given in Mr. H. St John Thackeray's valuable book *St Paul and Contemporary Jewish Thought*, pp. 172-179, where three parallel tables of their descriptions will be found. References to them in Christian apocryphal literature are collected in Dr Charles's *Book of the Secrets of Enoch* (from the Sclavonic), pp. xliv-xlvii. Hippolytus in his *Commentary on Daniel* (ed. Achelis, p. 96), referring to ... in the Benedicite, says: ... . Clement of Alexandria *(Strom,* iv. 25) says: ..., Origen *(c. Cels,* vi. 21) likewise mentions the Seven Heavens, but without committing himself to the exact number.

Irenaeus in I, i. 9 refers to the Valentinian teaching which identified the Seven Heavens with angels of varying degrees of power. In our passage he strangely connects the Seven Heavens with the Seven Gifts of the Spirit. We observe two peculiarities in his description. First, that, numbering from above downwards, he reckons the highest as the First Heaven: secondly, that his Seventh, or lowest, is the firmament. Evil is wholly excluded from these heavens: so it is in the *Ascension of Isaiah* (for which see Introd. p. 41), where however it is found in the firmament, which is not reckoned as one of the heavens.

The belief in the Seven Heavens soon came to be discredited; and it is curious to find a survival of it, due apparently to Irish influences, in the invocation of the *septem caelos* in a book of prayers of the seventh or eighth century (Brit. Mus. Reg. 2. A. xx, f. 47 *v.*).

27. [1] Compare the reason given by Justin Martyr *(Dial. 22)* for the worship in the Temple: ....

28. [2] Perhaps the text should be emended so as to give "operation " ....

29. [3] Or "ministrations " (= ... in Arm. version of i Cor. xii. 5).

30. Isa. xi. 2f.

31. [5] The heavens are enumerated from above, in order to correspond with the prophet's words and put Wisdom first and Fear of God last.

ADDITIONAL NOTE (p.151 of printed text): On p. 78, n. 5. Compare the fragment attributed to Victorinus of Pettau, printed by Routh, *Rell.* III, 458: "Summum ergo coelum sapientiae," etc. The common source maybe "the Elders" or Papias.

32. Ex. xxv. 40.

33. [4] The meaning is uncertain: the word means "daily, continual, perpetual"; but it is also used as an adverb. The German translations take it in the sense of "eternal" (sein ewiger Sohn). It renders dia_panto_j in Lev. xxiv. 2; and that may have been the original Greek in this passage. But even so it is not clear whether it is to be taken with "who is His Son," or with "is glorified"----For the Eternal Sonship we may compare III, xix. I: "existens semper apud Patrem; " and IV, xxxiv. 3: " semper cum Patre erat."

34. [5] Origen in his Commentary on *Romans* (III, § 8) interprets the two Cherubim over the mercy-seat as the Son and the Holy Spirit. In

De Principiis (I, Hi. 4, IV, iii. 26) he gives the same interpretation of the two Seraphim of Isa. vi. 3, saying that he received it from his Hebrew teacher: he adds that the same applies to the two living creatures of Hab. iii. 2 (LXX). Philo (*Vit. Mos.* iii. 8) had interpreted the two Cherubim as ..., the latter ku&rioj. This probably paved the way for Origen's interpretation.

35. Cf. Rev. v. 13.

36. [1] Elsewhere Irenaeus constantly speaks of the Son and the Spirit as the Hands of God: *see* Introd. p. 51.

37. [2] Equivalent to *plasma* or *plasmatio.*

38. [3] So both the German translations: but they transfer the words so as to link them with " this great created world." What we seem to want is, "to have all as his own," if the words can bear that meaning.

39. [1] For this function of angels cf. Papias, as quoted by Andreas *in Apocal.* c. 34, serm. 12: ...

40. [3] That Paradise was in a region outside this world is not quite distinctly stated here, but the opening words of c. 17 seem to support this view. The view of Irenaeus, however, is clearly given in V, v. 1: ... (Gen. ii. 8) . . . . He goes on to speak of this as the Paradise into which St Paul was caught up (2 Cor. xii. 4). Moreover he identifies it with the resting-place of just men, such as Enoch and Elijah. So in the Apocalypse of Peter the just are dwelling in a .... Irenaeus is silent as to whether Paradise is in the third heaven. But the Slavonic *Secrets of Enoch,* referred to above, places it there. In the shorter and apparently more original recension we read as follows (c. 8): "And the men removed me from that place, and brought me to the third heaven, and placed me in the midst of a garden; a place such as was never seen for the goodliness of its appearance. And every tree is beautiful, and every fruit ripe; all kinds of agreeable food springing up with every kind of fragrance. And (there are) four rivers flowing with a soft course; and every kind of thing good, that grows for food," etc. The Valentinians, according to Irenaeus (I, i. 9), placed Paradise ...

Comp. the Anaphora in the *Liturgy of St Basil* (Swainson, p. 80): ...

41. Gen. ii. 19.

42. Gen. ii. 18. As LXX.

43. Gen. ii. 21 ff.

44. [2] As LXX.

45. Gen. ii. 25.

46. Gen. ii. 16f.

47. [1] IV, lxvi, 2; ... V, xxiv. 4: ... Cf. Wisd. ii. 24: ...

48. [2] V, xxi. 2: "Satana enim verbum Hebraicum apostatam significat." Cf. Just. Mart. *Dial.* 103.

49. [3] Cf. Gen. iii. 24: ... . Perhaps "the way" comes from "the way of the tree of life " in the same verse.

50. Gen. iv. 1 f.

51. Gen. iv 25.

52. [1] This is from the Book of Enoch, to which Irenaeus also refers in IV, xxvii. 2. *Enoch* vii. 1: .... Tertullian makes use of the same passage: *De cultu fem.* i. 2, ii. 10 (ut Enoch refert).

53. [1] The Armenian corresponds to the Greek o(new&teroj (Gen. ix. 24). As there were three sons of Noah, the comparative causes difficulty. Origen took it as a superlative: for in later Greek (as in French) the comparative with the article is used as a superlative. He went on to argue that as Ham was not the youngest son of Noah, the word "son" was used for grandson, and that "Noah knew what his grandson (Canaan) had done to him": hence the curse falls on Canaan. This accorded with a tradition given him by his Hebrew teacher (*Comm. in Gen.* ix. 18; Lomm. viii, p. 65). The trouble arose from the fact that "the curse of Ham" was not pronounced on Ham, but on his son Canaan. Justin Martyr *(Dial.* 139) says that Noah

cursed his son's son; "for the prophetic Spirit would not curse his son, who had been blessed together with the other sons by God."

54. ¹ Irenaeus makes no difficulty about speaking of "the curse of Ham." It is clear that he had a text of the LXX, which enabled him to do so. The Hebrew of Gen. ix. 25 gives us: "Cursed be Canaan: a servant of servants shall he be unto his brethren." The LXX has: .. But some MSS (E and some cursives) read Xa&m for Xana&an. When pai=j was taken with the preceding word, Xa_m pai=j was no doubt intended to mean "the child of Ham," *i.e.* Canaan: it might however be understood as "Ham the child." So here the Armenian translator does not give the genitive case of Ham, but the nominative: and it would seem that he rightly interprets the meaning of Irenaeus.

55. Gen. ix. 25.

56. ² Irenaeus seems to have drawn on Acts ii. 9-11 to amplify his list.

57. ¹ The LXX reads *Canaan,* but one cursive has *Ham.*

58. Gen. ix. 26.

59. ² Here again the LXX reads *Canaan,* though E and other MSS. have *Ham.* The Arm. here has "he shall bless" for "he shall dwell "; but this is a slip, as appears from below.

60. Gen. ix. 27.

61. Ps. xix. 4.

62. ³ "The calling of the Gentiles," or, as we have it also here, " the calling from among the Gentiles," recurs in cc. 28, 41 *bis,* 42, 89, 91. I have noted it in the Armenian version of IV, xxxiv. 12, where however we find in the Greek..., and in the Latin .... I do not remember to have met with it elsewhere in the writings of Irenaeus, or in any earlier writer. In the fragments of Hippolytus on Gen. xlix (ed. Achelis, pp. 59 ff.) ... is found several times, and more than once ... occurs as a various reading. It is not found, however, in the corresponding comments in *The Blessings of Jacob* (Texte u. Unters. xxxviii. 1).

63. [1] With all the above cf. Just. M. *Dial.* 139.

64. Gen. ix. 14 f.

65. Gen. ix. i ff. [2] These last words are so quoted in V, xiv. 1. The LXX continues: .... This Irenaeus paraphrases; cf. c. II: "for (as) the image of God was man formed and set on the earth." That "the image of God is the Son" may be a reminiscence of Col. i. 15.

66. Gen. xi. 1.

67. [1] Lit. "was found" ....

68. [2] This is explained by the comment above (c. 21) on the blessing of Shem, which did not say "Blessed be Shem," but "Blessed be the Lord, the God of Shem"; meaning that God "should be to Shem a peculiar possession of worship."

69. Gen. xii. (1 Acts vii. 3).

70. [3] Heb. and LXX: "seventy and five."

71. Gen. xvii. 8.

72. Gen. xv. 5.

73. Gen. xv. 6; Rom. iv. 3.

74. [1] The Arm. has "uncircumcision" for "righteousness" by an oversight.

75. Rom. iv. 11.

76. Acts vii. 14.

77. [1] The same interpretation of Pascha, as if from pa&sxein is found in IV, xx. I: "cujus et diem passionis non ignoravit, sed figuratim praenuntiavit eum, Pascha nominans."

78. Ex xxxi. 18; xxxiv. 28

79. [1] "The finger of God" (Luke xi. 20) appears as "the Spirit of God
" in Matt. xii. 28. Cf. *Barn.* xiv. 3; and *Clem. Hom.* xi. 22, xvi. 12,
quoted in Introd. p. 53 n. 1.

80. [2] Num. xiii. 16 .... Justin Martyr *(Dial.* 75, 113) has much to say
on this change of name. Cf. *Barn.* xii. 8 f.

81. [1] Probably this represents .... Compare the brief clauses: "and this
came to pass " (c. 67), and "as indeed they have become" (c. 72); III,
vi. 4: "quod et erat." But it might be rendered, in conjunction with
the Name, " which was (given them) ": so the German translations
take it.

82. [1] Cf. the Greek fragment attributed to Irenaeus, Harvey II, p.
487, where we have ...: this fragment, however, is now shown to be
from Hippolytus On the Blessings of Moses *(Texte u. Unters.* N. F. XI,
la, p. 49). Cf. also IV, ii. 1: "Moyses igitur recapitulationem universae
legis ... in Deuteronomio faciens."

83. Deut. xxxii. 49 f.

84. Deut. xxxiv. 5

85. [1] Or "this present Jerusalem": perhaps representing ... (Gal. iv.
25).

86. [2] Cf. c. 51.

87. Eph. i. 10.

88. [3] For this double rendering see above c. 6.

89. [2] Cf. 2 Tim. i. 10: ...

90. John i. 14.

91. [1] Almost the same words are here used as in III, xxx. I.: ... Cf. III,
xix. 6: also Ephraim's Commentary on the Diatessaron (Moesinger, p.
21): "In Virginis conceptione disce quod qui sine conjugio Adamum
ex virginea terra protulit, is etiam Adamum secundum in utero

virginis formaverit." Cf. also Tertullian, *De carne Christi,* 17; Firmicus Maternus, *De errore prof. relig.,* 25.

92. Gen. ii. 5.

93. Gen. i. 26.

94. [4] The same parallel is worked out in III, xxxii. 1, and V, xix. 1. It is found earlier in Justin Martyr *(Dial.* 100), and later in Tertullian *(De carne Chr.* 17).

95. [1] Irenaeus is fond of referring to the sheep that was lost: see III, xx. 3, xxxii. 2, xxxvii. I; V, xii. 3, xv. 2.

96. [3] See above, c. 32.

97. Cf. I Cor. xv. 53.

98. [1] Cf. c. 68.

99. Isa. 1. 5 f.

100. Phil. ii. 8.

101. [2] V, xvii. 4: ... The Greek, preserved in a Catena, is here emended from the Latin and Armenian versions, both of which omit ...

102. [3] V, xviii. *2:* ... The thought is taken from Justin *(Ap.* I. 60)" who attributes to Plato the words: ... ... (cf. *Timaeus* 36 B.C.). See above, Introd. p. 29. Justin says that Plato misunderstanding the story of the Brazen Serpent, ...

103. Phil. ii. 15. Gen. xv. 6; cf. Rom. iv. 3. Gal.iii. ii; Rom. iv. 13. i Tim. i. 9.

104. [2] III, xxvi. 1: ... III, xi. 4, xvii. i, xxix. I. In all these places the phrase "eternal king" is used in connexion with this particular promise. The phrase also occurs in III, xx. 2, and below in cc. 56, 66, 95. Justin uses it several times *(Dial.* 34,36, 118, 135), but not in this connexion.

105. [1] Here and above I have used "body" as in A. V. for koili/a: but the strange argument is thus somewhat obscured. The words which immediately follow in the Armenian text may be more easily rendered in Latin: "*de fructu ventris tui,* quod est proprium feminae praegnantis: non de fructu lumborum, nec de fructu renum, quod est proprium viri generantis: ut declararet," etc. Almost the same words are found in III, xxvi. I: cf. also III, ix. 2: "ex fructu ventris David, id est, ex David virgine." The argument is used by Tertullian, *Adv. Marcion,* III, 20.

106. [2] The same word corresponds to "artifex" in the Arm. version of V, xv. 2, xxiv. 4: cf. III, xi. II: ..

107. [1] Cf. C. 39: *Barn.* V. 6: ...: and Hippolytus, *Apostolic Tradition,* in the Eucharistic Prayer: " ut resurrectionem manifestet "; and *Philos.* x. 33 (Connolly, *Texts and Studies,* VIII, 4. 166).

108. Rev. i. 5.

109. Amos ix. ii.

110. [2] Or "body": cf. c. 62.

111. Rev. i. 5.

112. Col. i. 18.

113. Isa. ix. 6.

114. [1] Cf. c. 97 (where however the Incarnation is in question), and the references there given.

115. [2] Or " fleshly": cf. I, ii. I: ...

116. [2] Cf. c. 21. The Arm. is obscure, perhaps corrupt.

117. [1] Cf. Just. M. *Ap.* 1. 32: ...

118. Gen. i. i.

119. [2] Lit. "the Armenian language."

120. ³ The Hebrew text has been corrupted in transmission: but it is plain that Irenaeus interpreted the first two words ("In the beginning created") as " In the beginning the Son." St Hilary, on Ps. ii. §2, says that *bresith* has three meanings, "in principio in capite, in filio "; but he prefers the first as the interpretation given by the LXX. See the note of the learned Dom Coustant, the Benedictine editor of St Hilary. See also Dr Harnack's notes in *Texte u. Unters.*, I, l.117ff. and xxxi, I. 60. In Clem. Alex. *Ed. Proph.* 4 we find as a comment on Gen. i. I, ...

121. ⁴ Ps. cx. 3, lxxii. 17. For this composite quotation from the Psalms, here attributed to Jeremiah, see Introd. p. 19 ff.

122. ⁵ For this quotation also see Introd. p. 22 f.

123. ⁶ This is probably a reference to Prov, viii. 22: ...

124. ¹ Justin (*Dial.* 88) quotes the Voice at the Baptism in the form " Thou art my Son, this day have I begotten thee " (Ps. ii. 7, and Luke iii. 22 in Codex Bezae, etc.). ...

125. John i. 1 ff.

126. Gen. xviii 1 ff.

127. Gen. xix. 24.

128. Gen. xxviii. 12 f.

129. ² The Arm. text has "from heaven to heaven" by oversight. That Jacob's Ladder signified the Cross was said by Justin (*Dial.* 86).

130. Acts vii. 49 (Isa. lxvi. i).

131. Isa. xl. 12.

132. Ex. iii. 7.

133. ³ V, xvii. 4: ...(where neither Lat. nor Arm. supports the inserted *Betas*): cf. c. 79. For this ... cf. *Barn.* XII. *2;* Just. M. *Dial.* 91, 112, 131.

134. Cf. I Cor. x. 4. Cf. Ex. xv. 27. I Cor. xiv. 20. Cf. Ex. xvii. 9 ff.

135. [3] Cf. Athan. *Orat.* i. 64: ...

136. Heb. i. 8 f. (Ps. xlv. 6f.).

137. [3] This is Justin's interpretation of the words: see *Dial.* 33...

138. [4] .. cf. *Barn.* XII, 11: so also many later writers.

139. Isa. xlv. 1.

140. Ps. ii. 7 f.

141. Ps. cx. 1. Isa. xlv. 1.

142. Ps. ii. 7.

143. [1] The subject is fully treated by Justin (*Ap.* I, 36 ff.): ...

144. [1] Here the quotation corresponds with Acts xiii. 47, as in Just. M. *Dial.* 121.

145. Isa. xlix. 5 f.

146. [2] Cf. c. 30. Justin says (*Dial.* 62): ...

147. [1] The construction of the Arm. is uncertain, but the general sense is plain. ..

148. Isa. vii. 14 ff.

149. [1] For comments on the rest of this chapter, see Introd. pp. 15 f.

150. Isa. lxi. 1.

151. [2] After the word "death " the Arm. has again "at that time."

152. Cf. Matt, i. 23.

153. [4] Or, perhaps," a cry of augury."

154. Isa. vii. 14.

155. [5] Cf. c. 71; and Just. M. *Ap.* I, 47... *Dial.* 118 . ...

156. Isa. lxvi. 7.

157. [2] The transposition of "son " and " child " would seem to be an oversight: see however Just. M. *Ap.* I, 35...: and note that the whole passage is quoted differently in c. 56 below.

158. Isa. ix. 6.

159. Gen. i. 26.

160. Isa. ix. 5 ff.

161. [3] The Arm. appears to mean "of the Risen One": but the text may be corrupt.

162. Gen. xlix. 10 f.

163. [1] The translation is uncertain. Cf. Justin, *ibid.:* ...

164. Cf. Ps. civ. 15. Isa. vii. 14. Isa. xxxv. 10. Isa. xi. 10. Num. xxiv. 17.

165. [4] So in III, ix. 2 ("dux").. The only other evidence for this seems to be Just. M. *Dial.* 106: LXX, ...

166. Cf. Matt, ii. 1-9.

167. [1] Cf. *Protevang. Jacobi* (cod. D): ...: *Opus Imperf. in Matth.* p. 30: "venit et stetit super caput pueri." Codex Bezae has ... (with *vet. lat.*).

168. [1] Lit. "with spirit through the lips," as in LXX.

169. Isa. xi. 1 ff.

170. [4] The Arm. means "with," not "by means of." Cf. Just. M. *Dial.* 86... the Rod from Jesse's root is there said to be Christ.

171. [5] Or "body."

172. [2] In V, xxxiii. 4 he discusses the same question and, while recognizing that some persons give a symbolical interpretation, he inclines to look for a literal fulfilment. Here also he finds room for both interpretations. The passage of Papias there quoted, as to the marvellous productivity of the millennial period, ends with the statement that the animals will live in peace and concord and in subjection to man. This explains the reference to the Elders in our text.

173. [1] The Arm. text as printed gives "in my name"; but by a different division of the letters we get " in one name."

174. [2] Cf. c. 38.

175. Amos ix. 11.

176. [3] Or " flesh"; and so throughout the passage.

177. [1] Cf. Wisd. ix. 15 (R. V.): "For a corruptible body weighs down the soul, and the earthly frame ... lieth heavy on a mind that is full of cares:" 2 Cor. v. I: 7) ...

178. [2] Matt. ii. 6 (Micah v. 2.) Irenaeus quotes the prophecy in the Matthaean form, which differs much from the LXX rendering. Moreover he agrees with Codex Bezae in reading ... Justin quotes the words twice in the Matthaean form, but with the ... *(Ap.* I, 34, *Dial.* 78).

179. [4] " My " for " thy " (LXX ...) by oversight. Part of the text is quoted in III, ix. 2. See also above, c. 36.

180. [1] Ps. cxxxii. 10 ff. The Arm. has "and their son for evermore," and nothing further.

181. [2] Matt. xxi. 5 (Isa. lxii. II; Zech. ix. 9). The passage is quoted in the Matthaean form, and ascribed to Isaiah from whom the first words come. In St Matthew's Gospel it is ascribed to "the prophet," though some codices insert "Zachariah." Justin quotes it differently, *Ap.* I, 35, *Dial.* 53.

182. [3] Cf. cc. 36, 56, 95.

183. Matt. viii. 17 (Isa. liii. 4).

184. Isa. xxix. 18.

185. Isa. xxxv. 3ff.

186. Isa. xxvi. 19.

187. [1] The Arm. text gives the passive ("be understood "); but doubtless the LXX ... was read: the difference is only in the final letter.

188. Isa. ii. 13 ff.

189. [2] The repetition in the Arm. of the word here rendered "tormented " suggests that the same Greek verb would underlie the words of the prophet ("was tormented for our sins") and of the psalmist ("And I was tormented"). But in the former case we and ..., and this verb does not occur in the LXX of the Psalms. Probably the reference is to Ps. xxxviii. 8 (9), ... Isa. liii. 4, 7. For the argument cf. Just. M. *Ap.* I, 35...

190. [1] Isa. i. 6. Cf. c. 34.

191. Lam. iii. 30.

192. Isa. liii. 5f.

193. [2] The Arm. word for "lamb " in this place *(amaru)* seems to be a Syriac loan-word: see the note in Dr. Weber's translation.

194. Isa. liii. 7. Isa. liii. 8.

195. Isa. liii. 8.

196. Lam. iv. 20.

197. [1] Or "flesh," as elsewhere.

198. [2] Cf. c. 59, *ad fin.*

199. [3] The words appear to mean literally: "the Spirit becoming as it were a shadow with glory and covering it (*or* him)."

200. [4] This is said of St Peter in Acts v. 15.

201. Isa. lvii. 1 f.

202. [1] The same point about "the Just" and "just men" is made by Justin (*Ap.* I, 48, *Dial.* 110).

203. Ps. xxi. 4.

204. Ps. iii. 5.

205. Ps. ii. 1 f.

206. [1] Pilate was procurator of Judaea for ten years (27-37). Claudius did not become emperor until A.D. 42. The statement here made is therefore inconsistent with the chronology of history: but it agrees with the view, expressed in II, xxxiii. 2ff., that our Lord reached *aetatem seniorem,* that is, an age between 40 and 50: a view which is largely based on John viii. 57: "Thou art not yet fifty years old, and hast thou seen Abraham? " For these words seemed to Irenaeus to show that He could not have been much less than fifty at the time when they were spoken. See C. H. Turner's art. "Chronology" in Hastings' *Dict. of the Bible.*

207. Cf. Acts iv. 25 ff.

208. [2] The Armenian is here uncertain.

209. [3] Cf. c. 64 for a similar oversight.

210. Lit. "for trembling." Ps. lxxxix. 39 ff.

211. [2] "Smite" is in the singular, as in cod. A of the LXX, which is here followed.

212. Zech. xiii. 7.

213. [3] Cf. c. 93, and IV, xxix. 5; "in duodecim prophetis Malachias." Often in Justin.

214. Hos. x. 6.

215. [4] The same interpretation is given by Justin *(Dial.* 103).

216. [1] This is one of the prophecies which Justin declared the Jews had erased from their Scriptures *(Dial.* 72) It is quoted several times by Irenaeus: III, xxii. 1 (as from Isaiah); IV, xxxvi. i (as from Jeremiah, to whom Justin had attributed it); 1. I (an allusion only); lv. 3 ("alii autem dicentes: Rememoratus . . . causam reddiderunt propter quam passus est haec omnia"); V, xxxi. I (with variations, and no name of author).

217. Isa. lxv. 2.

218. [2] Cf. c. 46: *Barn.* XII. 4: Just. M. *Ap.* I, 35.

219. Ps, xxii. 16.

220. [3] Ps. xxii. 14, 17. Ps. xxii. 20; cxix. 120; xxii. 16. " Nail my flesh " comes from the LXX. of Ps. cxix. 120, where A. V. has "My flesh trembleth for fear of thee." Cf. *Barn.* V, 13: ...

221. Deut. xxviii. 66.

222. Ps. xxii. 17 f.

223. Cf. John xix. 23 f.

224. Matt, xxvii. 9 f. (Zech. xi. 13).

225. Cf. Matt. xxvi. 15.

226. [4] In Matt. xxvi. 15 Cod. Bezae and some other authorities have ... for ... .

227. Cf. Matt, xxvii. 34. Joh. xix. 29.

228. Ps. lxix. 21.

229. Ps. lxviii. 17 f.

230. Eph. iv. 8.

231. Ps. xxiv. 7

232. ¹ Ps. xxiv. 8 ff.   Justin's interpretation *(Dial.* 36) makes the humble form of our Lord's humanity ... the reason why He is not at once recognized. The interpretation given by Irenaeus corresponds to that of the *Ascension of Isaiah:* see Introd. p. 43.

233. Ps. cx, 1.

234. Ps. xix. 6.

235. Rom. x. 15 (Isa. lii. 7).

236. Isa. ii. 3.

237. Ps. xix. 4.

238. Cf. Matt. vi. 7.

239. Rom. ix. 28 (Isa. X. 22 f.).

240. Rom. xiii. 10.

241. ¹ Matt. xxii. 37 f.; Mark xii. 30 f. For the abbreviation of the "First Commandment " cf. Just. M. *Dial.* 93. X .

242. Isa. l.8 f.; ii. 17.

243. Isa. lxv. 15 f.

244. Isa. lxiii. 9.

245. ² The word means more especially "to live in freedom."

246. Isa. xliii. 18ff.

247. Cf. Rom. vii. 6.

248. [5] Lit. "giving my laws"; cf. Heb. viii. 10.

249. Jer. xxxi. 31 ff.; Heb. viii. 8 ff.

250. [2] Or " hope ": and so twice below.

251. Isa. xvii. 7f.

252. [3] Or " manifest," as in the quotation below.

253. Isa. lxv. 1.

254. Rom. ix. 25 f. (Hos. ii. 23, i. 10).

255. Matt. iii. 9.

256. Ezek. xi. 19 f.

257. John i. 14.

258. [3] Both the German translations take the passage to mean: "granting many children to the Church, the assembly of the firstborn." But it is hard to get this out of the Armenian text, which has "first" and not "first-born." It seems certain that there is a contrast between "the Church" and "the first Synagogue" (whose husband was the Law, as is said below). The text can easily be amended so as to give the meaning required. Cf. IV, xlviii. i. f: "duae synagogae...fructificantes...filios vivos vivo Deo "; III, vi. i: " Ecclesia, haec enim est synagoga Dei." For the quotation and its interpretation cf. Just. M. *Ap.* I, 53.

259. Isa. liv. 1; Gal. iv. 27.

260. Cf. Deut. xxviii. 44. Deut. xxxii. 21; Rom. x. 19.

261. Cf. Jer. ii. 8.

262. [1] In the Arm. "who is" refers to "the Son,"

263. [2] Cf. 36, 56, 66.

264. [1] Dr Rendel Harris *(Testimonies* I, 66) has pointed out that this is a reminiscence of Polycarp, *Ep. ad Phil.* ...

265. Cf. Rom. xiii. 10.

266. i Cor. xiv. 20.

267. Ex. xx. 13 ff.; Deut. v. 17 ff.

268. Ex. xxi. 24.

269. [4] Just. M. *Dial.* 12...

270. Hos. vi. 6. Isa. lxvi. 3. Joel ii. 32. Cf. Acts iv. 12.

271. ADDITIONAL NOTE.----A new instalment has now appeared of the *Patrologia Orientalis* (XII. 5: Paris, 1919), containing a reprint of the Armenian text, with a translation into English by the discoverer, Ter-Mekerttschian, and Dr S. G. Wilson. This is followed by a much more accurate translation into French by the late Pere Barthoulout, S.J., formerly a missionary in Armenia. Among other valuable notes he points out that the opening words of c. 97 have been wrongly separated from the preceding chapter. The next sentence would then appear to mean: "He is separated and withdrawn from among men, and (yet) wheresoever," etc.

54043599R00040

Made in the USA
Middletown, DE
12 July 2019